The TOMATO Cookbook

Also by Roy F. Guste, Jr.
The 100 Greatest New Orleans Creole Recipes

The TOMATO Cookbook

Roy F. Guste, Jr.

PELICAN PUBLISHING COMPANY
Gretna 1995

*The word "Pelican" and the depiction of a pelican are trademarks
of Pelican Publishing Company, Inc.,
and are registered in the U.S. Patent and Trademark Office.*

Library of Congress Cataloging-in-Publication Data

Guste, Roy F.
    The tomato cookbook / Roy F. Guste, Jr.
       p. cm.
    Includes index.
    ISBN 1-56554-045-X
      1. Cookery (Tomatoes) I. Title.
  TX803.T6G87 1995
  641.6'5642—dc20   94-1488
                                            CIP

Manufactured in the United States of America

Published by Pelican Publishing Company, Inc.
1101 Monroe Street, Gretna, Louisiana 70053

For Allen, Althea, Andre, Antoine, Audrey, Barbara, Barbie,
Beatrice, Bebe, Becky, Bernard, Beth, Bette, Bev, Beverly, Billy,
Bitsie, Bobbie, Bobby, Bonnie, Bootsie, Britton, Buck, Buddy, Busta,
Butsie, Caesar, Carling, Carlos, Carlton, Carol, Caroline, Catherine,
Cathy, Cecil, Charles, Cheryl, Christine, Cindy, Claudia, Colette,
Collinet, Craig, Cybil, David, Dill, Dottie, Ed, Edward, Elizabeth, Ella,
Eugenie, Eve, Frank, Glade, Greeley, Greg, Grover, Henri, Hillary,
Hugh, Irle, Jack, Jackson, Janet, Jean, Jeff, Jem, Jessica, Jill, Jim,
Jimmy, Joe, Joel, John, Johnny, Jon, Jonathan, Jules, Julia, Julie,
Julot, Katherine, Ken, Kenny, Kermit, Kevin, Kurt, Larry, Leon,
Leonie, Louie, Louis, Maggie, Maise, Manon, Marc, Marda, Margaret,
Marie Louise, Marilyn, Mary, Maureen, Michael, Michelle, Mike,
Milburn, Mimi, Missy, Nancy, Narcisse, Nina, Palmer, Pam, Paul, Phil,
Preston, Rachel, Ralph, Ray, Rayme, Rick, Ricky, Robert, Roy, Ruthie,
Sam, Sandra, Scout, Sophie, Spencer, Stephanie, Stephen, Steve,
Stevie, Susan, Suzanne, Taylor, Terry, Tim, Tom, Tomate, Tommy,
Toto, Tric, Uwe, Vicky, Yvette, Yvonne,
and, of course, Bubba, Babe, and Boo.

Contents

Preface 9

Introduction..11

Beverages 17

Appetizers...27

Soups 43

Salads 57

Side Courses 73

Vegetables..95

Eggs 101

Seafood 109

Poultry..129

Meats 139

Sauces, Dressings, and Stocks..............147

Salsas and Condiments........................165

Muffins, Rolls, and Desserts 177

Index 188

Preface

Readers, cooks, and fellow culinarians:

This work is a living volume of selected recipes that together provide a broad but brief overview of the many ways that tomatoes are employed in world cuisines.

I say a living volume because I expect to revise and enlarge this work as the years pass, until it can be considered the definitive tomato cookbook. Perhaps this will be a lifetime project.

With this in mind, I invite you to assist me in the continued investigation and collection of tomato recipes, lore, and even graphics, and to send me your own recipes and information for possible inclusion in future works.

Merci, mes amis.

Roy F. Guste, Jr.

Please send correspondence in care of

Pelican Publishing Company, Inc.
P.O. Box 3110
Gretna, Louisiana 70054

Introduction

The tomato is one of the world's great culinary treasures. Born in the Americas, the tomato was a primary food source of the early inhabitants long before the Spanish arrived to take control of the land.

The Mexicans first cultivated the tomato, although the plant originated in the Peru-Ecuador region of the Americas. Before cultivation, the tomato grew as a weed, spreading throughout South and Central America. Because of its similarity to the Mexican tomatillo—the small, green, husk-covered vegetable resembling the tomato that the Mexicans had long-used as an essential ingredient in their cooking—the Mexicans easily adapted recipes to incorporate the tomato.

The name that we use for the fruit—yes, it is a fruit—comes from the Nahuatl Indian language word *tomatl. Lycopersicum esculentum* is the botanical name for the tomato. The tomato is a member of the Solanaceae group, or the nightshade family, which includes eggplant, Irish potatoes, and all peppers of the expansive *Capsicum genus*, which includes sweet bell peppers, pimentos, chili peppers, habanero peppers, jalapeño peppers, tabasco peppers, and cayenne peppers.

For many years after its discovery and its introduction into Europe, the tomato was thought to be poisonous, principally because of its membership in the Solanaceae family, which does include cultivars that are poisonous themselves, or whose leaves are poisonous. This relationship caused the Europeans great concern over its edibility and possible toxic content. Thus, the tomato met its first use as an ornamental shrub.

But the Europeans were not a people who would not investigate the tomato fully before passing it off as inedible. The tomato began to be eaten by adventurous "scientists" and their enlightened followers. In France, it was found to be not only edible, but (erroneously), also an aphrodisiac. Thus the French, as is their nature, began viewing the tomato as the miracle cure for maladies of love and as an agent to increase potency and dubbed the tomato the *pomme d'amour*, or "love apple."

It was, however, to be the eighteenth century before the tomato rooted firmly in the gastronomy of Europe.

All varieties of the tomato that we know today are far removed from its earliest cultivated ancestor. That tomato was a variety of cherry-type tomato, yellow in color, and quite small in relationship to the plump, round variety so familiar to us. This early tomato, *Lycopersicum cerasiforme*, is common in the Peru-Ecuador region, one of the three food baskets of the world.

For a very long time before the discovery of the New World by the Europeans, foods and spices had been both transported and transplanted by a series of sea routes and over dangerous and difficult land routes that made up the highway to Africa, India, and the East. Almost all of the foods that were common to India and the Mediterranean, two of the three food baskets of the world, had long been infused into each other's cuisines, as adaptation allowed. The remaining larder of foods, the third food basket of the world—Central and South America—still remained unknown to these worlds. These foods were to ignite an explosion of culinary artistry and experimentation in the wake of their discovery.

The tomato reached the Old World first in Spain where it was employed as an ornamental plant, and as in the Americas, was used as a cure for some disorders and as an aphrodisiac. It also began to claim its share of interest as a magical plant and was employed in the development of potions for use in magic.

In Italy, the foods chosen to be used in cookery, especially pasta, were simple, only waiting for the addition of an element such as the tomato to bring forward a marvelously tasting dish. Before the time of tomatoes, pasta was served with sauces made of turnip or carrot, or simply with a little grated cheese.

Pasta was also considered a dish for the poor—inexpensive, with an extended shelf life. It was eaten with the hands. It was because of the tomato sauce now added to the pasta to make it a more savory dish that the fork came into more general use.

Before this time, the fork was placed on the tables of the very wealthy more as a token of class rather than a necessity for proper dining. The fork that is used today was originally designed specifically for pasta with sauce.

The sudden infusion of the tomato sauce and the use of the newly discovered and imported foodstuffs of the Americas brought to the Italian table a considerable nutritional benefit, one that can only be paralleled with the twentieth century intro-duction of refrigeration into the household kitchen.

The tomato was first cultivated in France in the south, but soon gained enormous popularity in Paris on the very eve of the French Revolution. The blood-red color of the tomato was welcomed by the revolutionaries just as was their song, "La Marseil-laise," adopted as their battle cry.

Some historians believe that the tomato changed the world. Certainly, it was the combined group of New World foods—the tomato, squash, potato, corn, cacao, beans, peppers, etc.—that did. What existing world cuisine today does not employ some, if not all of these foods?

In America, it is almost impossible to think of our daily meals without the use of tomatoes, whether they are employed in sauces, salads, or anywhere we choose to place them in the meal.

The following is an analysis of the considerable nutritional benefits of the tomato:

1 whole fresh tomato	
Average weight:	123 grams, 4.34 ounces
Calories	24.0
Protein	1.09 grams
Carbohydrates	5.34 grams
Dietary fiber	1.80 grams
Fat—Total	0.260 grams
Saturated	0.037 grams
Monounsaturated	0.039 grams
Polyunsaturated	0.107 grams
Cholesterol	0 milligrams
Vitamin A	139 RE
Vitamin C	21.6 milligrams
Calcium	9.00 milligrams
Magnesium	14.0 milligrams
Phosphorus	28.0 milligrams
Potassium	255 milligrams
Sodium	10.0 milligrams
Percentage of calories:	
Protein	16 percent
Carbohydrates	76 percent
Fats	8 percent

Low in calories and almost devoid of fat, the tomato is both healthful and nutritious.

A single tomato contains forty percent of the recommended daily allowance of vitamin C, and twenty percent of the recommended daily allowance of vitamin A. Tomatoes are high in potassium and iron, but low in sodium. This is a most healthful combination.

The tomato is one of the great culinary treasures of the world: one that we are now on the road to finally fully recognizing.

The
TOMATO
Cookbook

BEVERAGES

The tomato lends itself quite liberally to a good number of popular beverages, many of them usually employing alcohol of some kind.

All of the recipes here can be made with great success without the addition of alcohol. So, enjoy, however you prefer your tomato cocktail.

SIMPLE RAW TOMATO JUICE

1 qt. skinned, seeded, and chopped tomatoes
Salt to taste

In a blender or food mill, process the prepared chopped tomatoes into a liquid. Salt to taste.

Strain the liquid through cheesecloth. Transfer the juice to a jar, cap, and refrigerate. Makes 1 quart.

Note: Be sure to retain all juices rendered in the skinning, seeding, and chopping of the tomatoes, especially the jelly around the seeds. It contains a good flavor and the highest content of vitamin C.

COOKED TOMATO JUICE

1 qt. skinned, seeded, and chopped tomatoes
2 ribs celery, chopped
1 tbsp. chopped parsley
Salt to taste

In a saucepan, combine the prepared tomatoes, celery, and parsley. Bring to a simmer and cook for 5-7 minutes. Season to taste with salt.

Transfer the mixture to a blender or food mill and process into a liquid. Strain the liquid through cheesecloth. Transfer the juice to a jar, cap, and refrigerate. Makes 1 quart.

Note: As in the preceeding recipe, be sure to retain all juices rendered in the skinning, seeding, and chopping of the tomatoes. It is most healthful.

TOMATO BEER

Some mornings it really does take a "hair of the dog" to get things moving again. My experience is that this rather refreshing morning starter, which is lighter in alcohol than a Bloody Mary, does the trick. It quenches the thirst and calms the stomach.

1 cup very cold, fresh tomato juice
(see Simple Raw Tomato Juice)
Dash hot sauce, optional
1 very cold beer of your choice

Fill a large glass or mug with ice to chill it thoroughly. Discard the ice and pour in the tomato juice. Add a dash of hot sauce if you so desire.

Next, pour in the beer slowly and carefully down the side of the glass to cause as little "head" to rise as possible. Makes 1 tall cocktail.

Drink freely as you would a beer.

Note: This is not a sipping cocktail. It is best in good, cold swallows to quench the morning thirst and ease other hangover discomforts.

TOMATO-CLAM COCKTAIL

¾ cup fresh tomato juice
(see Simple Raw Tomato Juice)
¼ cup clam juice
Juice from ¼ lemon
Dash hot sauce, optional
Salt to taste
Black pepper, freshly ground, to taste
1 rib celery or quarter (lengthwise)
of cucumber for garnish

Combine all of the ingredients except for the garnish in a cocktail shaker with ice, shake briefly, and pour into a double old-fashioned glass.

Garnish with a rib of celery or a quarter of a cucumber. Makes 1 cocktail.

BLOODY BULL

½ cup fresh tomato juice
   (see Simple Raw Tomato Juice)
⅓ cup beef bouillon or stock
2 oz. vodka, or less
1 tsp. freshly squeezed lemon juice
Dash Worcestershire sauce, or to taste
Dash Louisiana hot pepper sauce, or to taste
Salt to taste
Black pepper, freshly ground, to taste
½ rib celery or pickled string bean

In a cocktail shaker, combine the tomato juice, the beef bouillon, the vodka, the lemon juice, and a dash each, to taste, of Worcestershire and Louisiana hot pepper sauce. Season to taste with salt and freshly ground black pepper. Shake briefly.

Pour the cocktail over ice in a double old-fashioned glass and garnish with a half celery rib or pickled string bean. Makes 1 cocktail.

BLOODY MARY

1½ oz. vodka
5 oz. fresh tomato juice
   (see Simple Raw Tomato Juice)
1 tsp. lemon juice
Dash Worcestershire sauce
Dash Tabasco hot pepper sauce
Salt to taste
Black pepper, freshly ground, to taste
½ rib celery

In a cocktail shaker, combine the liquid ingredients with ice, salt and pepper to taste, and shake briefly. Pour into a cocktail glass and garnish with the celery as a stirrer. Makes 1 cocktail.

CAJUN BLOODY MARY

5 oz. fresh tomato juice (see Simple Raw Tomato Juice)
2 oz. pepper-flavored vodka
1 tbsp. lemon juice
Dash Worcestershire sauce
Several dashes Louisiana hot pepper sauce
Salt to taste
Black pepper, freshly ground, to taste
1 mild pickled jalapeño pepper for garnish

In a cocktail shaker, combine the fresh tomato juice, vodka, lemon juice, Worcestershire sauce, and Louisiana hot pepper sauce and shake briefly.

Pour the cocktail over ice in a double old-fashioned glass and season to taste with salt and freshly ground black pepper.

Cut a slit in the mild pickled jalapeño pepper and slip it onto the rim of the glass for garnish. Makes 1 cocktail.

Note: Unflavored vodka can be used in place of the pepper vodka.

CARIBBEAN BLOODY MARY

5 oz. fresh tomato juice (see Simple Raw Tomato Juice)
2 oz. rum
2 tsp. lime juice, freshly squeezed
Dash habanero hot pepper sauce, or to taste
Salt to taste
Black pepper, freshly ground, to taste
¼ lime

In a cocktail shaker, combine the fresh tomato juice, the rum, lime juice, hot pepper sauce, and salt and pepper with a few cubes of ice and shake briefly.

Pour the cocktail, ice included, into a cocktail glass and garnish with the lime quarter. Do not over-ice the Caribbean Bloody Mary. Ice cubes should merely be enough to float atop after shaking to chill. Makes 1 cocktail.

Note: Canned tomato juice can be used in place of the fresh.

The habanero hot pepper sauce is essential in this version of the Bloody Mary because it imparts the necessary island flavor of that particular pepper, the habanero pepper.

GULF COAST BLOODY MARY WITH HORSERADISH

The first time I ever enjoyed a Bloody Mary made according to this recipe was at the Broadwater Beach Hotel Bar in Biloxi, Mississippi, some twenty-five years ago. It was so delightfully different that I have since included it in the repertoire of drinks that I serve to my guests.

**5 oz. fresh tomato juice
(see Simple Raw Tomato Juice)
2 oz. vodka, or less
1 tsp. prepared horseradish
1 tsp. lemon juice
1 tsp. lime juice
Dash Worcestershire sauce
Dash Louisiana hot pepper sauce
Salt to taste
Black pepper, freshly ground, to taste
2 small radishes, brushed clean**

In a cocktail shaker, combine the fresh tomato juice, vodka, prepared horseradish, the lemon and lime juices, Worcestershire sauce, and Louisiana hot pepper sauce and shake briefly.

Pour the cocktail over ice in a double old-fashioned glass and season to taste with salt and freshly ground black pepper.

Cut a slit into the two radishes and slide them together onto the rim of the glass for garnish. Makes 1 cocktail.

CREOLE BLOODY MARY

5 oz. fresh tomato juice
   (see Simple Raw Tomato Juice)
2 oz. vodka, or less
1 tsp. Creole mustard
1 tsp. lemon juice, freshly squeezed
Dash Worcestershire sauce
Dash cayenne hot pepper sauce, or other
   Louisiana hot pepper sauce
Salt to taste
Black pepper, freshly ground, to taste
2 or 3 pickled okra for garnish

In a cocktail shaker, combine the fresh tomato juice, vodka, Creole mustard, lemon juice, Worcestershire sauce, and cayenne pepper sauce or other Louisiana hot pepper sauce and shake briefly.

Pour the cocktail over ice in a double old-fashioned glass and season to taste with salt and freshly ground black pepper.

Garnish the cocktail with several pickled okra. Makes 1 cocktail.

Note: The pickled okra are not absolutely necessary, but they are preferred. A celery rib will do in a pinch.

TEQUILA SANGRITA COCKTAIL

1½ cups orange juice, freshly squeezed
2 cups fresh tomato juice
   (see Simple Raw Tomato Juice)
¼ cup grenadine
½ cup freshly squeezed lime juice
Habanero hot pepper sauce to taste
Salt to taste
8 oz. tequila (½ pint)
1 lime, quartered

Combine the juices, grenadine, and seasonings; cover tightly; and refrigerate until well chilled. Chill the tequila at the same time in the freezer.

Mix the ingredients together in a pitcher and serve with or without ice, and place a lime wedge for garnish on the rim of each glass. Makes 4 cocktails.

Note: Again here the habanero hot pepper sauce is required over a Louisiana hot pepper sauce to get the proper taste. The habanero pepper is also called the Scotch-bonnet pepper.

MEXICAN BLOODY MARY

This recipe comes from Cancun on the Yucatan Peninsula of Mexico.

> **5 oz. fresh tomato juice**
>   **(see Simple Raw Tomato Juice)**
> **2 oz. tequila, or less**
> **1 tbsp. orange juice, freshly squeezed**
> **1 tsp. fresh lime juice**
> **1 tsp. minced fresh cilantro leaves**
> **Dash habanero hot pepper sauce, or to taste**
> **Salt to taste**
> **Black pepper, freshly ground, to taste**
> **Slice orange and lime for garnish**

In a cocktail shaker, combine the fresh tomato juice, tequila, the orange and lime juices, minced cilantro leaves, and habanero hot pepper sauce to taste and shake briefly.

Pour the cocktail over ice in a double old-fashioned glass and season to taste with salt and freshly ground black pepper.

Garnish the rim of the glass with a slice each of orange and lime. Makes 1 cocktail.

FLAMING TOMATO PUNCH

The idea of a Bloody Mary is no news to anyone, but the concept of a sweet Flaming Tomato Punch is considerably obscure. This recipe calls not only for vodka but also rum, which gives it a more tropical taste, although the recipe is derived from Italian cocktails.

1 lemon
1 cup water
½ lb. sugar
1 cup vodka
1 cup dark rum
1 cup fresh, unsalted tomato juice

Grate the zest from a lemon and mince it finely. Squeeze the juice from the lemon. Hold aside.

In a saucepan, heat the water and sugar until the sugar melts. Boil for about five minutes. Add the lemon zest and remove from the heat to cool.

When the sugar mixture is cooled, add the vodka, rum, tomato juice, and lemon juice.

Transfer the punch into tightly capped bottles until ready for use.

To serve the punch, warm it slightly in a bowl or saucepan. Pour approximately four ounces per serving into flameproof cups or glasses and carefully ignite with a flame. Serve while the punch is still flaming. The flame will soon die out as the alcohol is burned off. Makes 1 quart, or 8 4-oz. servings.

APPETIZERS

Although I will list a few dishes here as appetizers, the truth is that almost all of the dishes contained in this collection can be served as appetizers.

To distinguish the difference between an appetizer and a salad or a side course is purely subjective. Your own desired placement of any tomato dish in the meal is the most important determining factor.

BALTIC TOMATOES

4 medium tomatoes
Salt to taste
4 medium new potatoes
Enough salted water to cover
2 pickled herring fillets
8 cornichons
¼ cup Tomato Mayonnaise
Salt to taste
Black pepper, freshly ground, to taste
2 tbsp. red wine vinegar

Slice off the tops of the tomatoes and scoop out the insides. Season the interiors with salt. Invert the tomato shells on a plate to allow them to drain off any excess moisture.

In a saucepan, heat enough salted water to cover the potatoes. Boil them until they can be easily pierced through to their centers with the blade of a thin knife. Remove the potatoes from the cooking water to drain and cool.

Cut the pickled herring into small dice. Cut the cooled potatoes into small dice. Chop four of the cornichons.

In a bowl, combine the diced pickled herring and diced boiled new potatoes with the chopped cornichons. Blend this mixture with the Tomato Mayonnaise and season to taste with salt, if necessary, and freshly ground black pepper.

Sprinkle the interiors of the tomatoes shells with red wine vinegar and season with freshly ground black pepper. Spoon the herring-potato stuffing mixture into the seasoned shells and lay a small cornichon across the top of each tomato for garnish. Serves 4.

Note: If you choose not to use cornichons, which are small French pickles, you may substitute whatever gherkins you may have available. The dish will not be as delectable, but it is possible.

ROMA TOMATO RINGS
STUFFED WITH CREAM CHEESE

6 large ripe Roma tomatoes
¾ cup cream cheese
1 tbsp. Tomato Paste
1 tsp. fresh lemon juice
½ tsp. salt
¼ tsp. white pepper
¼ tsp. hot sauce, or to taste
1 tsp. bell pepper, minced
1 tsp. celery, minced
1 tsp. green onion, minced
1 tsp. pimento, minced
1 tsp. parsley, minced
1 tsp. capers, minced
1 tsp. green olives, minced
1 tsp. anchovy fillet, minced, or anchovy paste
Additional capers, pimento dice,
** or olive slices for garnish.**

Cut out the stems of the Roma tomatoes and use the handle of a teaspoon to remove the seeds. Discard the seeds.

In a bowl, thoroughly combine the remaining ingredients except for garnish ingredients. Cover and chill in the refrigerator.

Stir the cream cheese filling mixture to loosen it a bit and spoon it into the tomatoes. If you have a pastry bag, it would be handy to fill the bag with the cream cheese mixture and squeeze it into the tomatoes. Be sure that the tomatoes are completely filled and that there are no air pockets. Cover the stuffed tomatoes and refrigerate.

When preparing to serve the stuffed Roma tomatoes, remove them from the refrigerator and place them on a cutting board. Using a very sharp knife, wet with water to slice the tomatoes crosswise into rounds approximately ½" thick. Place the slices on a serving plate.

Garnish the center of each tomato round with a caper, small dice of pimento, or olive slice. Serves 4, or makes approximately 2 dozen pieces.

Note: This is a tasty little appetizer that can also be enjoyed with cocktails. They can also be used as a garnish in a salad or to decorate the border of a cold stuffed tomato dish.

TOMATOES BEAUREGARD

16 cherry tomatoes
Salt to taste
White pepper to taste
Tarragon vinegar to taste
1 7-oz. can tuna, packed in oil or water, drained
2 tbsp. butter, softened
2 tbsp. mayonnaise
Juice from 1 lemon
4 lettuce leaves, or 1 cup chopped lettuce
1 lemon, quartered

Slice off and reserve the tops of the cherry tomatoes. Scoop out and reserve the insides for stocks or sauces. Season the interiors with salt, white pepper, and tarragon vinegar. Set aside.

In a bowl, fold together the tuna fish with the softened butter and mayonnaise. Blend in the lemon juice and season to taste with salt and white pepper. Spoon the tuna mixture into the cherry tomato shells. Top with the reserved tomato top slices.

Place a lettuce leaf, or make a bed of chopped lettuce, on each of the four chilled salad plates. Serve the tomatoes on the lettuce. Garnish each plate with a lemon quarter. Serves 4; allows 4 pieces each.

SARDINES ROVIGO CANAPE

In earlier times in New Orleans it was both popular as well as "chic," to serve dishes and recipes employing products shipped overseas from Europe. One of the most popular items was sardines.

If you are a sardine lover, this might interest you.

> **5" center piece stale French bread,**
>   **or 4 slices other bread**
> **1 clove crushed garlic**
> **3 tbsp. olive oil**
> **2 dozen canned sardines**
> **½ cup Tomato Sauce**
> **¼ tsp. ground, dried sage leaves**
> **Salt to taste**
> **White pepper to taste**
> **½ small green bell pepper, thinly julienned**
> **1 hard-boiled egg, chopped**

Using a serrated knife, cut the French bread at an angle into 8 elongated oval-shaped slices, approximately ½" thick. If you are using another bread, trim the crust off the slices and halve the slices diagonally. Rub the bread slices on each side with the clove of crushed garlic.

In a wide skillet or sauté pan, heat the olive oil and fry the bread slices on both sides until lightly browned and crisp. Lay these fried bread "croutons" in a single layer on a plate and cover each with three sardines, or enough to fairly cover each crouton.

Combine the Tomato Sauce with the sage, season to taste with salt and white pepper, and nap the sardines with the sauce. Sprinkle the sardine canapés with the julienned green bell pepper and the chopped hard-boiled egg. Serve at room temperature. Serves 4; allows 2 pieces per person.

Note: The herb—sage, here—can be varied to any other that suits you: basil, oregano, thyme, etc. Fresh herbs in place of the dried are nice when you have them available. Use three times the measure of fresh herbs when substituting for dried herbs.

If you are an anchovy lover, like I am, substitute anchovies for the sardines. You will probably need 2 anchovy fillets in place of each sardine.

COLD TOMATO MOUSSE

1 pkg. plain gelatin
¼ cup cold water
2 tbsp. butter
4 cups coarsely chopped tomato pulp
1 cup Velouté Sauce
1 tsp. salt
¼ tsp. white pepper
⅛ tsp. cayenne pepper
1 tbsp. lemon juice
½ cup whipping cream

In a small bowl, stir the gelatin together with the water and set aside to allow the gelatin to soften.

In a saucepan, melt the butter and cook the tomato pulp until it is fairly dried out of its liquids. Add the softened gelatin and water and stir until all is well combined and the gelatin particles are all completely dissolved. Add the Velouté Sauce and season with salt, white pepper, and cayenne pepper.

Press the mixture through a fine sieve, or process it in a food processor or blender until completely smooth. Transfer to a mixing bowl and allow to cool. Add the lemon juice.

In a chilled bowl, whip the cold whipping cream until it stands in soft peaks. Fold the whipped cream into the cooled tomato mixture. Spoon the mixture into 4 individual cups or molds, or into a single, larger soufflé dish. Cover with plastic wrap and refrigerate for two hours, or until well set.

Turn out of the molds to serve. If you have used the single soufflé dish you can cut the tomato mousse into slices to serve. To loosen the mousse from the molds, simply dip them in hot water for a few seconds, neatly loosen the sides with a thin bladed knife, turn over onto a plate, and shake downward. You will hear the mousse "plop" from the mold onto the plate. Serves 4-6.

Note: This is an excellent accompaniment to hot or cold fish dishes, especially if you have made the Velouté with a fish or shellfish stock.

Cold chicken or chicken salad would also be a prime entree with which to serve this mousse. In this case, you would want to have made the Velouté with a chicken stock.

This base recipe is unembellished with any strong herb or spice flavors, but you may want to add your preferred herbs or spices to develop the depth of the recipe further.

TOMATO FRIBOURG

16 cherry tomatoes
Salt to taste
Black pepper, freshly ground, to taste
1 minced green onion
3½ tbsp. minced chives
⅔ cup small-diced, unpeeled, boiled new potatoes
⅔ cup grated Gruyère cheese
½ cup Tomato Mayonnaise

Slice off the stem end of the tomatoes, scoop out the insides, and season their interiors with salt and freshly ground black pepper.

In a bowl, combine the minced green onion, 2 tbsp. minced chives, the potatoes, the grated Gruyère cheese, and the Tomato Mayonnaise. Season to taste with salt and freshly ground black pepper.

Fill the cherry tomato shells with the mixture and sprinkle the tops with the remaining 1½ tbsp. minced chives. Serves 4; allows 4 tomatoes per person.

Note: Although the Tomato Mayonnaise adds to the recipe, it is not essential and can be replaced with plain mayonnaise.

CEVICHE

2 large tomatoes, chopped
2 habanero chili peppers, stemmed, seeded, and minced
1 large onion, chopped
2 large cloves garlic, minced
1 cup lime juice, freshly squeezed
¼ cup olive oil
¼ cup fresh cilantro leaves, minced
½ tsp. salt, or to taste
1 lb. skinned very fresh fish fillets
4 lettuce leaves

THE TOMATO COOKBOOK

In a bowl, combine the chopped tomatoes with the habanero chilies, onion, and garlic. Stir in the lime juice, olive oil, and cilantro. Season with salt.

Cut the fish fillets into bite-sized pieces and fold them into the other ingredients in the bowl. Be sure that they are completely covered by the ingredients and the liquids. Cover the bowl with plastic wrap and refrigerate for at least three hours. The fish will "cook" and become opaque as it marinates. Stir the fish around in the bowl once or twice during the marinating period to be sure all pieces are well exposed to the marinade.

The ceviche is done when the fish pieces are opaque all the way through. Adjust salt if desired. Serve the ceviche in glass dessert dishes or parfait glasses lined with lettuce leaves. Serves 4.

Note: Jalapeño peppers can be used in place of the habaneros. The amount of peppers used should be adjusted to suit your own tastes.

TOMATO BEAULIEU

4 medium ripe tomatoes, stemmed
Salt to taste
2 7-oz. cans tuna, packed in oil or water, drained
2 tbsp. Tomato Butter
2 tbsp. Tomato Mayonnaise
Juice from 1 lemon
White pepper to taste
1 hard-boiled egg
4 black olives, pitted

Halve the tomatoes lengthwise from top to bottom, salt them, and place them cut-side down on a plate to drain off any excess moisture.

In a bowl, fold together the tuna fish with the Tomato Butter and Tomato Mayonnaise. Blend in the lemon juice and season to taste with salt and white pepper. Spoon the tuna mixture into the tomato shells.

Shell and chop the hard-boiled egg and sprinkle it over the stuffed tomatoes. Garnish the top of each tomato half with a pitted black olive. Serves 4.

TOMATO GUACAMOLE

2 large ripe tomatoes, stemmed, seeded, and finely chopped
1 medium onion, chopped
1 fresh jalapeño pepper, seeded and finely minced
1 clove garlic, minced
¼ cup minced cilantro, or to taste
2 medium avocados
Salt to taste
1 tbsp. lime juice, freshly squeezed

In a bowl, combine the tomatoes, onion, jalapeño, garlic, and cilantro.

Prepare the avocado near the time it is to be served. Cut it lengthwise through to the pit and turn the two halves to loosen them from each other. Remove and discard the pits. Remove the avocado meat from the skins, chop it roughly, and add it to the other ingredients.

With a wooden spoon, stir the mixture together and mash the avocado meat until you have a mass of guacamole. Season with salt to your taste and add the lime juice. Serve immediately as an appetizer, or with chips as a dip. It can be stored briefly if plastic wrap is pressed against the top of the guacamole to protect it from the air. Serves 4.

Note: This recipe should not be prepared until near the time it is to be served. The initial steps of prepping the vegetables other than the avocados can be done, but the avocado should not be prepped until only a half hour before serving or the flesh will darken.

BAKED OYSTERS THERMIDOR

This is a recipe that was invented by my great-grandfather, Jules Alciatore, at Antoine's restaurant in the latter part of the nineteenth century.

2 dozen raw oysters on the half-shell
6 aluminum or tin pie pans filled with rock salt
(approximately 1 cup of rock salt per pan)
2 dozen Roma tomatoes
Salt to taste
Black pepper, freshly ground, to taste
Red wine vinegar
2 cups Cocktail Sauce
6 strips good bacon, cut into 4 pieces each

Preheat the oven to 400 degrees.

Set the oysters aside and make sure their shells are clean. Arrange the oyster half-shells in a circle on four rock salt-filled pie pans, six shells per pan. Cut the Roma tomatoes in half lengthwise and flatten the halves out. Place a tomato half, skin side down, on each of the oyster shells. Season the tomatoes with salt, freshly ground black pepper, and a sprinkle of red wine vinegar. Top each seasoned tomato half with a raw oyster. Place the pans to bake in the oven for 5 minutes, or until the edges begin to curl on the oysters and some of the liquids have been released from both the tomatoes and the oysters. Remove the pans of oysters from the oven.

Using a spoon, nap the oysters with the Cocktail Sauce and top each sauced oyster with a piece of bacon. Return to the oven. Cook for 5-7 minutes more, or until the bacon is cooked and the sauce is slightly browned. Serve immediately. Serves 4; allows 6 oysters per person.

Note: The idea of the salt-filled pie plates is an old one begun at Antoine's restaurant that has been used in New Orleans for many years to help hold the heat in the oysters between the kitchen and the table, and while the oysters are being eaten. It works, although it becomes somewhat cumbersome for the home cook. The recipe can be made without the rock salt.

CRABMEAT BEIGNETS WITH TOMATO SAUCE

1 tbsp. butter
1 large onion, finely chopped
4 cloves garlic, minced
½ cup chicken stock
1 bay leaf
6 whole ripe tomatoes, peeled, seeded,
  and chopped
2 tbsp. Tomato Paste
Salt to taste
White pepper to taste
½ cup flour
1 tbsp. baking powder
2 green onions, white part only, minced
3 tbsp. minced pimento
2 cloves garlic, minced
1 cup water
1 tbsp. olive oil
8 oz. crabmeat
1 tsp. salt
½ tsp. Tabasco sauce
Oil for frying

In a saucepan, heat the butter and sauté the onion and garlic until they become translucent, about 2 minutes. Add the chicken stock, bay leaf, tomatoes, and Tomato Paste. Simmer for 15 minutes and season to taste with salt and white pepper. Remove the bay leaf and puree the sauce in a blender. Keep the sauce warm.

In a bowl, combine the flour, baking powder, green onions, pimento, garlic, water, olive oil, crabmeat, salt, and Tabasco sauce. Cover the bowl with a damp towel and set it aside in a warm place for 30 minutes. Mix again and drop tablespoonfuls of the mixture into oil heated to 375 degrees in a cast-iron skillet. Fry until the beignets are lightly browned on both sides. Drain on paper. Serve the beignets with the warm tomato sauce spooned over them. Serves 6; allows 4 beignets per person.

TOMATO SHRIMP REMOULADE

4 large ripe tomatoes
Salt to taste
White pepper to taste
1/3 cup Creole mustard
1/3 cup light olive oil
2 tbsp. lemon juice
1 tbsp. paprika
1 tsp. salt
1/4 tsp. cayenne pepper
4 green onions, minced
2 ribs celery, minced
2 tbsp. minced parsley
1 lb. medium chilled boiled shrimp, peeled
   and deveined
2 cups chopped lettuce
2 lemons, halved

Cut off the tops of the tomatoes and remove the seeds and most of the pulp with a spoon. As you do this, be sure to scoop out one nicely rounded ball of pulp (as melon balls) from each tomato to use as garnish. Discard the seeds and the extra pulp. Sprinkle the interiors of the tomato shells with salt and white pepper. Turn the tomatoes upside down on a plate to drain off any excess moisture.

In a bowl, blend the Creole mustard, olive oil, lemon juice, paprika, salt, and cayenne pepper. Fold in the minced greens and boiled shrimp. Cover tightly and chill for 2-3 hours. To serve, divide up the chopped lettuce onto four individual chilled salad plates and spoon out the Shrimp Remoulade into the tomato shells. Top each with the reserved tomato balls and garnish with lemon halves. Serves 4.

Note: It is imperative that your ingredients are fresh and that the minced greens have a perceivable crunch.

The shrimp must have a bite and not be overcooked and soggy. Holding the shrimp in the sauce for too long will cause them to toughen.

TOMATO CRABMEAT RAVIGOTE

6 large Creole tomatoes
Salt to taste
White pepper to taste

Cut off the tops of the tomatoes and remove the seeds and most of the pulp with a spoon. As you do this, be sure to scoop out one nicely rounded ball of pulp (as for melon balls) from each tomato to use as garnish. Sprinkle the interiors of the tomato shells with salt and white pepper. Turn the tomatoes upside down on a plate to drain off any excess moisture.

CRAB RAVIGOTE

1 whole large egg
½ tsp. salt
¼ tsp. ground white pepper
⅛ tsp. cayenne pepper
2 tbsp. lemon juice
1 cup peanut oil
3 anchovy fillets, minced
2 green onions, minced
1½ tbsp. minced red pimento
1½ tbsp. minced green bell pepper
1 lb. lump crabmeat
Lettuce leaves for garnish
1 cup Vinaigrette Sauce

In a bowl, begin to make the Crab Ravigote by beating the egg, salt, ground white pepper, and cayenne pepper together with 1 tbsp. lemon juice. Briskly whisk in the oil, 1 tsp. at a time, until you have added ¼ cup and the mixture is beginning to emulsify. Continue whisking in the remainder of the oil 1 tbsp. at a time until you have added ½ cup. Now add the remaining 1 tbsp. lemon juice and beat in the rest of the oil 1 tbsp. at a time. Blend in the anchovy fillets, green onions, red pimento, and green bell pepper. Carefully fold in the crabmeat. Work it only enough for the sauce to be well distributed and all the crabmeat lumps to be well coated.

Fill each tomato with ½ cup Crab Ravigote and top with a ball of pulp. Chill the tomatoes in the refrigerator. To serve, place each tomato on a lettuce leaf and pour the Vinaigrette Sauce over it. Serves 6.

Note: The name comes from the French *ravigoter*, which means "to enliven or invigorate." The dish can be served as an entree in the summer for a cool light lunch.

Chilled, peeled boiled shrimp and crayfish can be used in place of, and in the same quantity as, the crabmeat. They each make an excellent ravigote.

SOUPS

The numerous recipes included in the many cuisines around the world for tomato-based soups could fill a volume of their own.

This brief listing includes selections designed to offer an overview of some of the ways tomatoes are used in soup and to suggest ideas for you to create your own variations.

TOMATO, MANGO, AND AVOCADO GAZPACHO

1 large very ripe tomato
1 small ripe mango
1 medium avocado
1 small sweet green bell pepper
1 small red onion
1 cup tomato juice
1 cup unsweetened pineapple juice
Juice of 2 limes
¼ cup minced fresh cilantro leaves
Salt to taste
Black pepper, freshly ground, to taste
1 tsp. hot sauce, habanero pepper,
  or Louisiana hot sauce

Skin, seed, and chop the tomato. Peel and seed the mango and avocado, and cut them into very small dice. Stem, seed, and finely chop the sweet green bell pepper. Skin and finely chop the red onion.

In a bowl, combine the tomato, mango, avocado, bell pepper, and red onion. Blend in the tomato juice, pineapple juice, and lime juice. Add the cilantro and season with salt and freshly ground black pepper. Add the hot sauce, using more or less to suit your taste. Cover and refrigerate for several hours or overnight. Serves 4.

Note: The first warm days of summer always produce in me a craving for light, tasty foods—what one might call "beach" cuisine. This tropical version of gazpacho has the addition of the tart sweetness of pineapple juice and the luscious mango fruit, along with the rich, velvety textured avocado.

BRAZILIAN CHICKEN AND TOMATO SOUP

2½ qt. chicken stock or water
2½ lb. chicken
6 medium tomatoes, skinned, seeded, and chopped
1 medium onion, skinned and chopped
1 rib celery, minced
1 large clove garlic, minced
2 tbsp. minced parsley
1 tbsp. minced cilantro
2 bay leaves
2 large carrots, cut into ½" dice
½ cup white rice, uncooked
Salt to taste
Black pepper, freshly ground, to taste

In a soup pot, add the chicken stock or water, and then add the whole chicken, tomatoes, onion, celery, garlic, parsley, cilantro, and bay leaves. Bring to a boil, cover, and lower the heat to cook at a simmer for one hour.

Carefully transfer the cooked whole chicken to a plate and remove all meat from the carcass. Rough chop the chicken meat and hold aside. Discard the bones.

Remove the two bay leaves and press the soup and the vegetables through a strainer, tamis, or process in batches in a blender or food processor. The vegetables should to be completely pureed into the soup liquor.

Return the soup to the pot and add the chopped chicken meat, carrots, and raw rice and season to taste with salt and freshly ground black pepper. Bring to a gentle boil and cook for thirty minutes more. Serves 4-6 generously.

Note: If the soup becomes too thick, add more stock or water.

The addition of a squeeze of lime added at the end of cooking gives a nice finish on the tongue.

Of course, a minced hot pepper can be added to raise the heat index.

This chicken and tomato soup concept comes from Brazil, where it is called *Canja*. The Portuguese culinary influence is apparent in this dish.

LOUISIANA TOMATO BISQUE

4 tbsp. butter
4 tbsp. flour
1 medium yellow onion, chopped
4 green onions, chopped
2 cloves garlic, chopped
1 stalk celery, chopped
1 qt. chicken stock
8 large ripe tomatoes, skinned, seeded,
 and chopped
2 tbsp. Tomato Paste
1 tbsp. chopped parsley
¼ tsp. thyme
2 bay leaves
4 whole cloves
Salt to taste
Black pepper, freshly ground, to taste
¼ tsp. cayenne pepper
Tomato Bisque Dumplings

Melt the butter in a heavy saucepan and stir in the flour. Cook this mixture, the roux, over moderate heat and stir regularly to ensure even cooking and to prevent burning for 5-7 minutes, or until the roux has acquired a brown color. Add the yellow onion, green onions, garlic, and celery and continue cooking until the vegetables have browned. Add the chicken stock, tomatoes, Tomato Paste, parsley, and seasonings. Cover and simmer gently for 1 hour.

Pass the bisque through a strainer and return it to the saucepan, adjust seasonings if necessary, and simmer for 15 more minutes. To serve the bisque, ladle it into soup bowls and garnish each serving with Tomato Bisque Dumplings. Serves 4-6.

Note: A Louisiana bisque is something quite different than that which you might find in other parts of the United States or in France. Ours is hearty and thick, dark and delicious, as opposed to the light-colored cream bisques one might be more accustomed to finding elsewhere.

TOMATO BISQUE DUMPLINGS

These dumplings are an important factor in elevating an already excellent dish from simply a good bisque to a dish of considerably more complex character and interest.

In a crayfish bisque, the heads of the crayfish would be stuffed and served in the soup as garnish. Here, we make a similar garnish using a kind of tomato stuffing to simulate the "heads."

2 tbsp. butter
½ small yellow onion, minced
1 green onion, minced
¼ cup minced celery
1 clove garlic, minced
1 tbsp. minced parsley
¼ tsp. thyme
1½ cups French bread crumbs
1 cup tomato puree
1 tsp. Tomato Paste
½ tsp. salt, or to taste
¼ tsp. powdered white pepper, or to taste
¼ tsp. cayenne pepper
1 medium egg

Preheat oven to 350 degrees.

In a heavy skillet, heat the butter and sauté the yellow onion, green onion, celery, garlic, parsley, and thyme for two minutes or until they become limp. Add 1 cup of the bread crumbs, the tomato puree, and Tomato Paste. Season with salt, white pepper, and cayenne pepper. Cook together until most of the liquid has been reduced and the mixture becomes dry enough to form into shapes, about 8 minutes. Remove from the heat. When the stuffing is cooled slightly, beat the egg and fold it in.

Using the measure of a rounded tablespoon, use your hands to roll the stuffing into egg-shaped "dumplings." Roll the dumplings in the remaining bread crumbs. Place the tomato dumplings on a greased baking sheet and bake in the preheated, 350-degree oven for about 12 minutes. Hold aside warm until the bisque is served. To serve, ladle the bisque into bowls and lay the tomato dumplings gently on the surface of the soup as garnish. Serves 4-6.

TOMATO AND CRAB BISQUE

6 ripe medium tomatoes
½ cup butter
½ cup flour
½ bunch green onions, chopped
1 qt. hot chicken or shellfish stock
1 qt. half & half
Salt to taste
White pepper to taste
¼ tsp. cayenne pepper, or a pinch
1 lb. crabmeat

Skin and seed the tomatoes, reserving any juice resulting from the process. Discard the seeds. Chop up the tomato pulp and hold aside with the tomato juice.

Melt the butter in a heavy saucepan and blend in the flour. Cook together for 3 minutes, or until the flour/butter mixture comes to a boil and you can smell the change from the smell of raw flour to the "bready" aroma that the flour acquires as this blend becomes the "roux." Do not let this roux color any darker than a pale, buttery color. Fold in the green onions and stir while cooking for about 2 minutes, or until the green onions are softened but not yet beginning to brown. Slowly whisk in the hot chicken or shellfish stock. Be very sure that there are no lumps in the texture of the soup. Bring to a boil.

Add the half & half and the reserved, chopped tomato pulp and juice. Bring the soup to a boil and turn down to a low simmer. Season to taste with salt and white pepper, and add the cayenne pepper. Simmer, uncovered, for 20 minutes. Just before serving, carefully fold in the crabmeat without allowing it to break up too much. Adjust seasoning to taste. Heat for just a minute more, only as long as it takes for the crabmeat to become well heated, and serve. Serves 4-6.

Note: Crayfish, shrimp, or oysters make delicious bisques with this recipe as variations to the crabmeat. If raw shrimp or oysters are used, be sure to simmer the soup long enough to cook them thoroughly, yet not overly so.

TOMATO AND EGGPLANT BISQUE

1 strip bacon, minced
1 large onion, skinned and rough-chopped
4 medium tomatoes, skinned, seeded, and chopped
1 small eggplant, skinned and chopped
2 cloves garlic, chopped
2 cups chicken stock or tomato juice
1 cup heavy cream
2 bay leaves
½ tsp. turmeric
½ tsp. minced lemon zest
⅛ tsp. cayenne pepper
Salt to taste
Black pepper, freshly ground, to taste
1 tbsp. freshly squeezed lemon juice
2 minced green onions

In a saucepan or soup pot, render the fat from the minced bacon and sauté the onions until they become soft. Add the other ingredients except the salt, pepper, lemon juice, and green onions; bring to a boil; turn down to a simmer; and cook for about 45 minutes. Season to taste with salt and freshly ground black pepper. Transfer the soup to a blender container and process into a liquid. Return to the pot and adjust seasonings, if desired. Just before serving, add the lemon juice to the bisque. Ladle the bisque out into bowls and garnish with chopped green onions. Serves 4.

Note: Adjust thickness of the bisque with additional stock, tomato juice, or water. The bisque should be quite thick.

TOMATO CREAM BISQUE WITH SHERRY

½ cup butter
½ cup flour
1 qt. tomato juice
1 cup whipping cream
¼ cup dry sherry
4 medium tomatoes, peeled, seeded
   and finely chopped
1 tsp. salt, or to taste
¼ tsp. ground white pepper
¼ tsp. cayenne pepper
1 tbsp. minced parsley

In a saucepan, or soup pot, melt the butter and blend in the flour. Cook together for three minutes, without coloring the roux. Whisk in the tomato juice and simmer for five minutes. Add the whipping cream, sherry, and tomatoes. Season to taste with salt, white pepper, and cayenne pepper. Bring the bisque to a simmer, and cook for about thirty minutes. Adjust seasonings if necessary. Serve the bisque garnished with chopped parsley. Serves 4-6.

COLD TOMATO AND SWEET POTATO SOUP

2 cups chopped tomato pulp
2 cups cooked mashed sweet potatoes,
   without skin
1 cup heavy cream
1 cup chicken stock
2 tbsp. butter
4 green onions, white only, chopped
1 tbsp. chopped parsley
Salt to taste
White pepper to taste
1 tbsp. chopped cilantro

In a saucepan, combine the tomato pulp with the sweet potatoes, heavy cream, chicken stock, butter, white of the green onions, and parsley. Bring to a boil, turn down to a simmer, cover, and cook for 20 minutes. Season to taste with salt and white pepper. Just before serving, garnish with chopped cilantro. Serve hot or chilled. Serves 4.

MANHATTAN CLAM CHOWDER

2 strips bacon, minced
¾ cup chopped onions
2 tbsp. flour
1 cup hot clam juice
2 cups chopped tomato meat
1 small rib celery, minced
3 cloves garlic, minced
1 cup tomato puree
1 cup tomato juice
2 bay leaves
¼ tsp. dried thyme
1 cup chopped clams
Salt to taste
Black pepper, freshly ground, to taste
1 tsp. Louisiana hot sauce, or to your taste
2 tsp. lemon juice, freshly squeezed
1 tbsp. chopped parsley

In a saucepan, heat the minced bacon until it is cooked and all the fat has been rendered. Add the onions and brown them lightly. Stir in the flour and cook together for one minute. Add the hot clam juice, tomato, celery, garlic, tomato puree, tomato juice, bay leaves, and thyme. Cover and simmer for fifteen minutes. Add the chopped clams, season to taste with salt and freshly ground black pepper, and add the hot sauce, to taste. Simmer until the minced clams are tender. Just before serving, stir in the lemon juice and chopped parsley. Serves 4.

THE TOMATO COOKBOOK

Note: Hot buttered and toasted French bread rounds, oyster crackers, or even saltines go well with the chowder.

You could add a cup of small, diced, boiled new potatoes, including skin, to the chowder to give it a more hearty consistency.

This soup makes a fine oyster chowder when oysters are used in place of the clams.

If the chowder becomes too thick, thin it with a little water.

WEST AFRICAN FISH, TOMATO, AND PEPPER SOUP

4 cups fish or chicken stock
4 tomatoes, skinned, seeded, and chopped
1 medium onion, chopped
2 tbsp. minced parsley
2 fresh hot red peppers, seeded and minced
2 cloves garlic, minced
2 bay leaves
1 tsp. dried thyme
1½ lb. raw boneless fish, diced
Salt to taste

In a saucepan, combine the fish or chicken stock with the tomatoes, onion, parsley, red peppers, garlic, bay leaves, and thyme. Bring to a boil, lower to a simmer, cover, and cook for 20 minutes. Add fish and simmer for ten minutes, or until fish is cooked and tender. Adjust seasonings, salting to taste if necessary, and serve. Serves 4.

Note: It is common in West African cookery to find soups and fish dishes prepared with hot peppers for seasoning. The peppers used in African cooking are strains of those brought from the Americas hundreds of years ago, now developed into African peppers of their own type. Small hot red peppers or red jalapeños will suffice. Or, you may want to use habanero peppers.

Any fresh fish can be used in this soup, as well as chicken.

NIGERIAN TOMATO AND PUMPKIN SEED SOUP

¾ **cup roasted pumpkin seeds**
½ **lb. chicken meat**
½ **lb. beef brisket**
¼ **cup peanut oil**
4 medium tomatoes, skinned and seeded
1 medium onion, chopped
1 hot red chili pepper (or jalapeño),
  seeded and chopped
2 cloves garlic, chopped
1 cup Tomato Sauce
1½ **cups tomato juice or water**
1 lb. fresh spinach, cleaned and chopped
¼ **lb. smoked herring or other smoked fish, diced**
Salt to taste
Black pepper, freshly ground, to taste
2 cups hot cooked brown rice

In a blender, process the pumpkin seeds to a powder or paste, depending on the moisture in the seeds. Cut the chicken and brisket into bite-sized dice. Heat the peanut oil in a saucepan or skillet and fry the chicken and meat until browned.

In a blender or food processor, process the tomatoes, onion, red chili pepper, and garlic into a puree. Pour it into the pan and add the Tomato Sauce, tomato juice or water, spinach, and fish and season to taste with salt and freshly ground black pepper. Simmer for ten minutes, add ground pumpkin seeds, and simmer for ten more minutes. Serve with cooked brown rice. Serves 4.

Note: In Nigeria this soup is also made from egusi seeds, which are difficult to come by. Use egusi seeds if you can find them, otherwise, the pumpkin seeds make a fine soup.

BLACK BEAN AND TOMATO SOUP

2 cups dry black beans
Enough water to cover
2 cups tomato meat
1 large onion, chopped
2 cloves garlic, minced
1 tsp. chili
¼ tsp. cumin
¼ tsp. curry
¼ tsp. ground coriander
⅛ tsp. cayenne pepper
1 cup chicken stock
Salt to taste
Juice from 1 small lime
2 tbsp. minced cilantro
2 green onions, minced

Cook the black beans in water until they are of a relatively soft consistency, one and one-half to two hours. Add water as needed during the cooking. Add the tomato meat, onion, garlic, chili, cumin, curry, coriander, cayenne pepper, and chicken stock. Bring to a boil and simmer for thirty minutes.

Puree the soup in a blender, return to the pot, and bring to a boil. Season to taste with salt. Adjust seasonings, if necessary, and stir in the lime juice. Garnish with minced cilantro and green onion. Serve. Serves 6.

CANTONESE TOMATO AND BEEF SOUP

4 medium tomatoes, skinned, halved, and seeded
4 oz. flank steak, or other beef steak
1 tbsp. soy sauce
1 tbsp. sherry
1 tsp. cornstarch
1 tsp. sesame oil
⅛ tsp. ground white pepper
2 tbsp. peanut oil
1 whole raw egg
1 tsp. minced fresh ginger
4 cups Beef Stock
Salt to taste
1 green onion, chopped

Cut each tomato half into four wedges. Using a very sharp knife, slice the beef into paper-thin pieces and transfer them to a small bowl. Add the soy, sherry, cornstarch, sesame oil, white pepper, and 1 tbsp. peanut oil. Mix well together.

In another small bowl, beat the egg briefly. Heat a saucepan until it is hot and add the remaining tablespoon peanut oil. Sauté the ginger until it browns. Add the sliced tomatoes and sauté for one minute. Add the Beef Stock, bring to a boil, and cook for two minutes. Add the paper-thin beef slices and bring the liquid back to a boil. Remove the pot from the heat. Pour in the beaten, raw egg in a thin stream and let it cook in the hot soup for about 30 seconds. Stir the cooked egg around in the soup to disperse it. Salt to taste, if necessary, and serve garnished with chopped green onion. Serves 4.

Note: Because of their proximity to the early trade routes, the Cantonese were the first Chinese to receive the tomato. This recipe is an example of how they have included it in their own cuisine.

SALADS

In the salad is probably where most of us grew up having the better part of our tomatoes.

In New Orleans, where we boast about the semiannual availability of one of the world's finest tomatoes, the Creole, there is much ado about salad tomatoes. Sliced, wedged, skinned, or chopped, they can be found anywhere a salad is served.

These representative selections are intended to offer alternate recipes, as well as traditional salads, that employ the tomato.

ANDALUSIAN TOMATO AND RICE SALAD

1½ cups cooked white rice, chilled
½ cup Tomatette Dressing
2 tbsp. minced white onion
1½ tbsp. minced parsley
1 clove garlic, pressed
5 medium-sized tomatoes
1 medium-sized green bell pepper, stemmed,
**   seeded, and skinned**
Salt to taste
Black pepper, freshly ground, to taste
2 green onions, chopped
½ tsp. paprika

Make sure that the cooked rice has been refrigerated for two hours, or is well chilled. In a salad bowl, combine the rice with the Tomatette Dressing, white onion, parsley, and pressed garlic. Toss all together until well mixed. Skin, seed, and dice three of the tomatoes. The remaining two tomatoes should be stemmed and sliced crosswise into ¼" thick rounds. Dice the green bell pepper. Add the diced tomatoes and bell peppers to the salad bowl and toss again until all ingredients are well distributed.

To serve the salad, line four chilled salad plates with the sliced rounds of tomato, so that they overlap one another in a circular fashion. Season with salt and freshly ground black pepper. Spoon the rice salad mixture into mounds on the tomato-lined plates. Garnish the salads with chopped green onion and sprinkle with paprika. Serves 4.

Note: Andalusia is the ancient name—from the Arabic *al-Andalus*, or "country of the Vandals"—of the southern most region of Spain, which now is divided into several provinces including Cadiz, Cordoba, Granada, and Seville.

CARIBBEAN CURRIED TOMATO, CORN, ORANGE, AND ONION SALAD

2 medium tomatoes, stemmed
2 small oranges
1 small red onion, peeled
1½ cups cooked corn kernels
Salt to taste
Black pepper, freshly ground, to taste
½-¾ cup Caribbean Curry-Lime Dressing
   (recipe follows)

Cut the tomatoes into ½" dice. Peel the oranges and separate or cut them into eight sections each, remove and discard the seeds, and reserve the juice that is released in the process. Cut the red onion in half from top to bottom, and then cut the two halves crosswise into paper-thin slices.

Put the tomatoes, orange sections, red onion, and corn kernels in a salad bowl. Add the reserved orange juice. Season lightly with salt and freshly ground black pepper. Toss the salad to mix the vegetables, and then add the Caribbean Curry-Lime Dressing. Toss the salad again until all is well coated with the dressing and serve out onto chilled salad plates. Serves 4.

Note: This salad is one that I first enjoyed in the Yucatan paradise of Akumal. Akumal is a small, quiet little stop along the edge of the Caribbean sea, south of Cancun as you head toward Tulum and then onto Belize.

It was a palapa open-air beach restaurant that served only grilled fresh-caught *huachinango*—snapper—and the most delicious roasted free-range chickens, all with garlic butter wherein the garlic was cooked in relatively large dice, mild flavored, and crunchy to the bite.

Before each entree this salad would be served. The Yucatecan family of owners all worked diligently in their own sense of time: the children delivered the cervezas and margaritas, Papa acted as host and waiter, and Mama banged away in the sad, makeshift little kitchen, the food from which would put the grandest culinary "laboratories" to shame.

It is not uncommon for me to attempt to repeat the fine meal I had at this little palapa restaurant, where the sand of the beach and the azure-blue waves glowed in the August moonlight. But, as delicious as my rendition is, it never quite matches that in Akumal.

CARIBBEAN CURRY-LIME DRESSING

½ cup peanut oil, or corn oil
3 tbsp. fresh lime juice
1 tsp. minced cilantro
1 tsp. curry powder
1 tsp. chili powder
1 tsp. habanero hot pepper sauce
1 tsp. salt
½ tsp. powdered mustard
¼ tsp. white pepper

In a small bowl, combine the peanut oil and lime juice by pouring the lime juice into the bowl first and slowly whisking in the peanut oil in a thin stream until all is added and emulsified. Add the cilantro, curry powder, chili powder, habanero hot pepper sauce, salt, powdered mustard, and white pepper. Whisk all together until the salt is completely dissolved. Makes ¾ cup.

Note: The use of a pepper sauce made from the habanero pepper is important. The flavor of this common Caribbean pepper is quite different from cayenne or tabasco peppers, so the sauces made from cayenne, tabasco, or other peppers— Louisiana hot sauces—will not deliver the exotic Caribbean flavor desired here.

If you are using a mildly hot habanero pepper sauce, you can use more in the dressing and attain a richer pepper flavor without too much hotness.

CARIBBEAN FISH, TOMATO, AVOCADO, AND GRAPEFRUIT SALAD

1 lb. chilled cooked fish fillets
Juice of 1 lemon
1 egg
½ cup cider vinegar
1 cup olive oil
1 tsp. sugar
¾ tsp. salt
¼ tsp. dry mustard
⅛ tsp. cayenne pepper
¼ tsp. black pepper
1 small head of romaine lettuce,
    leaves washed and prepped
2 medium tomatoes, skinned and sliced
1 small avocado, peeled and sliced lengthwise
1 grapefruit, peeled and sectioned
4 black olives

In a bowl, break the cold cooked fish fillets apart into bite-sized pieces. Sprinkle with the juice of a lemon, cover, and hold aside. Place the egg, vinegar, olive oil, sugar, salt, mustard, cayenne pepper, and black pepper in a blender and process until emulsified. Cover and refrigerate dressing.

Line four plates with the lettuce leaves. Top with the tomato slices. Place the avocado slices and grapefruit sections in a star pattern over the tomato. Spoon the prepared fish into the center of the avocado-grapefruit star. Pour the dressing over the salads. Garnish the centers with black olives. Serves 4.

TOMATOES STUFFED WITH CHICKEN AND MUSHROOMS

4 medium tomatoes
Salt to taste
1 cup diced fresh mushrooms
1 cup diced cooked chicken
½ cup Tomato Mayonnaise
1 tbsp. fresh lemon juice
White pepper to taste
Hot sauce to taste
Red wine vinegar to taste
¼ sweet green pepper, julienned
4 lettuce leaves
1 lemon, quartered

Slice off the top of the tomatoes. Scoop out the interiors to create tomato shells, reserving the pulp for sauces or stocks. Sprinkle the interior walls of the tomato shells with salt and arrange them cut-side down on a plate to drain off any excess moisture.

In a bowl, combine the diced mushrooms with the chicken and fold in the Tomato Mayonnaise. Stir in the fresh lemon juice and season to taste with salt, white pepper, and your choice of hot sauce.

Turn the drained tomato shells over and season the insides with white pepper and red wine vinegar. Spoon the chicken-mushroom stuffing into the shells. Arrange the julienned sweet green pepper strips over the tops of the tomatoes. Place the stuffed tomatoes on lettuce leaves on four chilled salad plates and garnish the plates with a lemon quarter. Serves 4.

ROMA TOMATO AND EGG SALAD

8 Roma tomatoes, washed and stemmed
8 hard-boiled eggs, shelled
Salt to taste
Black pepper, freshly ground, to taste
½ cup Tomatette Dressing
2 chopped green onions

Choose tomatoes that are not much wider than an egg. Slice the tomatoes crosswise into ¼" thick slices. Slice the hard-boiled eggs crosswise into ¼" thick rounds.

Arrange the tomato and egg slices alternatingly and overlapping at the edges in a circle on four chilled salad plates. Season lightly with salt and freshly ground black pepper. Spoon the Tomatette Dressing over the tomato and egg slices and garnish with chopped green onions. Serves 4.

Note: Any salad dressing can be used here. Vary your choice at different servings.

CHILLED EGG-STUFFED TOMATOES

4 medium tomatoes, washed and stemmed
6 large hard-boiled eggs, shelled
¼ cup Tomato Mayonnaise, or Mayonnaise
½ rib celery, minced
6 pitted black olives, minced
4 anchovy fillets, minced
1 tbsp. capers, minced
1 green onion, minced
Salt to taste
White pepper to taste

Hollow out the tomatoes, reserve the meat, and set it aside. Rough-chop the hard-boiled eggs and combine them with the Tomato Mayonnaise, celery, black olives, anchovy fillets, capers, and green onion. Chop the reserved tomato meat and add to the mixture. Season with salt and white pepper. Fill the tomato shells with the mixture. Serve. Serves 4.

Note: A Tomatette Dressing, or other dressing, can be poured over the stuffed tomatoes for additional flavor.

CREOLE CHICKEN AND TOMATO SALAD

2 cups diced cooked chicken
2 cups chopped tomatoes
2 tbsp. Creole mustard
¼ cup olive oil
2 tbsp. red wine vinegar
Salt to taste
Black pepper, freshly ground, to taste
4 lettuce leaves, washed
2 hard-boiled eggs, shelled and halved
1 lemon, quartered

In a bowl, combine the chicken and tomatoes. In another small bowl, beat the Creole mustard, olive oil, and red wine vinegar together to make the dressing. Season the dressing with salt and freshly ground black pepper. Toss the chicken and tomato mixture together with the dressing.

To serve the salads, spoon the mixture out onto cold salad plates lined with lettuce leaves. Top each salad with a half hard-boiled egg, and serve with a lemon quarter as garnish. Serves 4.

INDIAN TOMATO, RED ONION, AND GINGER SALAD

4 large ripe tomatoes, washed, stemmed,
**   and sliced crosswise into ½" thick rounds**
1 medium red onion, skinned and thinly sliced
Salt to taste
Black pepper, freshly ground, to taste
1 tbsp. grated fresh ginger
½-¾ cup Tomatette Dressing
½ tsp. curry powder

Arrange the sliced tomatoes in a circle, edges overlapping, on four chilled salad plates. Sprinkle the onion slices over tomatoes. Season with salt and freshly ground black pepper. Stir the grated ginger into the Tomatette Dressing along with the curry powder. Pour the ginger-curry-Tomatette Dressing over the salads and serve. Serves 4.

TOMATO SALAD WITH TOMATETTE DRESSING

4 medium, ripe tomatoes
1 medium onion, thinly sliced
Salt to taste
Black pepper, freshly ground, to taste
½ cup Tomatette Dressing
1 tbsp. chopped parsley

Cut the tomatoes crosswise into ¼" thick rounds. Arrange the rounds in close circles, edges overlapping, on four chilled salad plates. Scatter the thinly sliced onion over the tomatoes. Season the tomatoes and onions with salt and freshly ground black pepper. Pour over them the Tomatette Dressing and garnish with the chopped parsley. Serves 4.

YUGOSLAVIAN TOMATO AND PEPPER SALAD WITH GOAT CHEESE

**4 medium tomatoes, stemmed and sliced vertically
   into 8 wedges each**
**2 roasted medium-sized sweet green bell peppers,
   seeded, skinned, and cut vertically into 8 strips each**
**1 medium red onion, sliced vertically into 8 wedges
   and pulled apart**
**1 large mild red or green chili pepper, stemmed, seeded,
   ribbed, and sliced into thin strips**
½-¾ cup Tomatette Dressing
Salt to taste
Black pepper, freshly ground, to taste
4 lettuce leaves, washed
¾ cup crumbled goat cheese

In a bowl, combine the tomatoes, sweet green bell peppers, and the red onion with the mild red or green chili pepper. Pour in the Tomatette Dressing and toss the salad. Season to taste with salt and freshly ground black pepper. Serve the salad on a lettuce leaf on each of four chilled salad plates and top with the crumbled goat cheese. Serves 4.

*Note: T*his salad is a specialty of the region of Serbia, in what was formerly Yugoslavia. That area is a tomato-producing region.

TOMATO, AVOCADO, AND RED ONION SALAD WITH RUSSIAN TOMATO DRESSING

2 large avocadoes
2 large tomatoes
1 medium red onion
Salt to taste
Black pepper, freshly ground, to taste
1 cup Russian Tomato Dressing (recipe follows)
4 tsp. red lumpfish roe (caviar)

Peel the avocadoes and halve them lengthwise. Remove and discard the pit. Slice the avocado halves into ¼" slices lengthwise. Remove and discard the stems from the tomatoes and halve them top to bottom. Slice the tomato halves—again top to bottom—in ¼" slices. Peel the red onion and halve it top to bottom. Cut it top to bottom into paper-thin slices.

Divide the ingredients into four equal portions. Begin the assembly of the salads by first arranging a layer of avocado slices in a fan formation, wide end toward the outside rim of the plates. Next comes a layer of sliced red onions and then a layer of tomato slices. Season the vegetables lightly with salt and freshly ground black pepper. Nap with the Russian Tomato Dressing. Garnish the center of each salad with 1 tsp. red lumpfish roe. Serves 4.

Note: Black lumpfish or whitefish roe can be used in the place of the red lumpfish roe. They are the same product differing only in coloration. Or, for an even more extravagant salad, use real sturgeon caviar, or the less expensive red salmon caviar.

Louisiana is now producing, seasonally, a gaspurgou caviar that is quite acceptable and would do nicely in this salad with some fine Creole tomatoes, and maybe even sweet Vidalia onions—when available—in the place of the red onions.

This is a delightful salad that runs more toward haute cuisine than many others in this collection. The use of the red lumpfish roe adds an elegance that is most unexpected and enjoyable.

RUSSIAN TOMATO DRESSING

½ cup Tomato Mayonnaise
½ cup Tomato Catsup
2 tbsp. minced celery
2 tbsp. minced green onions
1 tbsp. minced parsley
¼ tsp. white pepper
¼ cup red lumpfish roe

In a small bowl, fold the Tomato Mayonnaise together with the Tomato Catsup. Add the minced celery, green onions, and parsley and blend all together well. Season with white pepper. Add the red lumpfish roe and continue to fold all together well. Be careful not to crush the roe eggs. Makes approximately 1½ cups.

Note: Salt is already in the Tomato Mayonnaise and the Tomato Catsup, and the lumpfish roe is heavily salted: there should be no need for additional salt in this dressing.

Of course, you can make this dressing very quickly from regular commercial mayonnaise and ketchup, which reduces the difficulty of preparation and time involved in the original dressing recipe considerably. You may even prefer the taste of the dressing made with commercial products, because you are already familiar with their taste.

This dressing is called Russian because of the lumpfish roe. I use the red-colored lumpfish roe in this recipe, but black lumpfish roe can be used as well, and it offers a nice contrast to the dressing's pink color. You can also use real sturgeon caviar, or the now seasonably available Louisiana caviar from gaspergou for a more haute cuisine recipe.

TOMATO BALL SALAD

6 large tomatoes
Salt to taste
Black pepper, freshly ground, to taste
1 cup chopped green onions
3 ribs celery, finely chopped
1 tbsp. red wine vinegar
1 tsp. Louisiana hot sauce
4 anchovy fillets, minced
1 cup Tomatette Dressing

Slice one of the tomatoes crosswise into four rounds. Place the rounds of tomato on chilled salad plates. Sprinkle the slices with salt and freshly ground black pepper. Skin and seed the five remaining tomatoes and chop the pulp. Combine the tomato pulp with the green onions, celery, red wine vinegar, hot sauce, and anchovy fillets. Use your clean hands to form the mixture into four balls and press tightly to allow the mixture to hold itself together. Place the tomato balls on the prepared tomato rounds. Spoon on the Tomatette Dressing and serve very cold. Serves 4.

Note: It may happen that you must wrap the tomato mixture in cheesecloth and squeeze out the excess liquid in order for the mixture to maintain a ball shape. Use the liquid that is released; add it to the Tomatette Dressing that is served over the salad.

Although somewhat more complicated than many of the other dishes presented herein, this salad is well worth the trouble. It is a clever presentation of the tomato that incorporates good flavors and is a delight to the eye when it is served.

SPANISH TOMATOES

4 large ripe tomatoes, chilled
Salt to taste
Black pepper, freshly ground, to taste
2 tbsp. olive oil
1 medium onion, chopped
½ small green bell pepper, chopped
2 green onions, chopped
1 small clove garlic, chopped
2 cups cold cooked white rice
¾ cup Tomato Mayonnaise
4 lettuce leaves
1 lemon, quartered

Cut out the stems of the tomatoes, making a round hole a diameter just large enough to scoop out the seeds with a teaspoon. Remove the seeds and season the insides of the tomatoes with salt and freshly ground black pepper. Set the tomato shells hole-side down on a plate to drain off any excess moisture.

In a sauté pan, heat the olive oil and sauté the onion, green bell pepper, green onions, and garlic until the vegetables are limp but have not yet begun to color. Remove from heat and allow to cool.

In a bowl, add the cold rice and blend it with the cooked vegetable mixture. Blend in ½ cup of the Tomato Mayonnaise, and reserve the remainder to top the tomatoes. Season to taste with more salt and freshly ground black pepper. Fill the tomato shells with the rice mixture. Chill in the refrigerator for one hour, or until ready to be served.

To serve, place a lettuce leaf on each of four chilled salad plates and set a tomato on each leaf. Spoon the remaining Tomato Mayonnaise over the holes in the tomato tops. Garnish with lemon quarters. Serves 4.

Note: The addition of a dash or two of Louisiana hot sauce to the rice stuffing gives this recipe a nice bite.

You may want to use other rices than plain white rice—say, popcorn rice, brown rice, yellow rice, or even a wild and white rice mixture.

The lettuce leaf garnish can be of any lettuce that fits the plate. Chopped lettuce may also be used.

ROASTED TOMATO SALAD WITH TARRAGON

4 large Roasted Tomatoes
Salt to taste
Black pepper, freshly ground, to taste
½ cup tarragon vinegar
4 lettuce leaves
1 small red onion, chopped
1 tbsp. fresh minced tarragon leaves

Having already skinned the Roasted Tomatoes, slice them into six or eight wedges each, season with salt and freshly ground black pepper. Place them in a bowl with the tarragon vinegar to marinate for a half hour in the refrigerator.

Arrange the tomato slices on lettuce leaves on four chilled salad plates, sprinkle with the chopped red onion, dribble over the marinating juices and garnish with the minced tarragon leaves. Serves 4.

TOMATO SALAD
WITH OLIVE-ANCHOVY DRESSING

½ cup pitted black calamata olives
6 anchovy fillets
1 tbsp. capers
¼ cup fruity green olive oil
¼ cup red wine vinegar
1 tsp. salt
¼ tsp. black pepper, freshly ground,
  plus more to taste
4 large chilled tomatoes, sliced
1 large French schallot, minced
Black olives for garnish

In a blender container, combine the pitted black calamata olives with the anchovy fillets, capers, olive oil, red wine vinegar, salt, and ¼ tsp. freshly ground black pepper. Process the ingredients into a liquid. Hold aside. Slice the tomatoes into ½" rounds and arrange them on chilled salad plates. Season lightly with black pepper. Spoon the salad dressing over the tomatoes and sprinkle with minced schallot. Garnish with black olives. Serves 4.

NIGERIAN TOMATO AND FRUIT SALAD

2 medium ripe tomatoes
2 medium bananas
2 small mangoes, skinned and seeded
1 cup diced fresh pineapple
Juice from 1 lime
1 cup coconut milk, fresh or canned
¼ cup sugar
½ cup shredded coconut

Peel and cube the tomatoes, bananas, and mangoes and combine in a bowl with the diced pineapple. Combine the lime juice with the coconut milk and sugar. Stir until the sugar is dissolved. Pour this liquid mixture over the fruit, cover and refrigerate for one hour to macerate. To serve, toss the salad in the juices, then add the shredded coconut and toss again. Spoon out into chilled salad bowls. Serves 4.

SIDE
COURSES

More often than in salads, we find the tomato as a side course or vegetable course served with the entree of a meal.

The following list of recipes will offer a few old favorites as well as some choices from other countries. Enjoy them all and serve them with your own entree recipes that you feel are best accompanied by these selections.

THE TOMATO COOKBOOK

BROILED TOMATOES WITH BREAD CRUMBS

4 medium tomatoes
4 tbsp. butter
Salt to taste
Black pepper, freshly ground, to taste
1 cup bread crumbs

Wash the tomatoes, cut out the stem, and cut crosswise into four rounds each. In a skillet, heat the butter and sauté the tomato slices briefly for just a few seconds on each side. Remove to a baking dish. Season with salt and freshly ground black pepper and sprinkle with the bread crumbs. Place the tomatoes under a broiler for 5 minutes to brown the tops. Serves 4.

TOMATOES JEANNETTE

6" length of stale French bread, or 12 slices other bread
4 tbsp. butter
2-3 large tomatoes, depending on their size
Salt to taste
Black pepper, freshly ground, to taste
1 tsp. paprika
½ tsp. cayenne pepper
¾ cup grated Parmesan cheese

Slice the stale French bread into ½" thick rounds and fry them in butter until lightly browned on both sides to make croutons. Slice the tomatoes crosswise into ½" thick rounds and place a slice on each of the twelve fried bread croutons. Season the tomatoes with salt, freshly ground black pepper, paprika, a pinch of cayenne pepper, and sprinkle about 1 tbsp. grated Parmesan cheese on each. Place under the broiler until the cheese is melted and begins to brown. Serve two pieces per person. Serves 6.

Note: One of the earliest cookbooks that claimed to be of New Orleans origin was one called "Mademoiselle Jeannette." There is some question, however, as to whether the book originated in New Orleans, or was printed in Paris and sent here as merely a simple guide to basic French cookery. This recipe is named for the author of that work.

BROILED TOMATOES WITH BLACK OLIVES
AND ROMANO CHEESE

4 medium tomatoes
2 tbsp. olive oil
2 cloves garlic, pressed
Salt to taste
Black pepper, freshly ground, to taste
½ cup black olives, pitted and minced
½ cup grated Romano cheese
1 tbsp. minced parsley

Preheat broiler. Slice tomatoes in half. Arrange cut-side up on a cookie sheet or broiler pan. Combine the olive oil and pressed garlic. Dribble it over the tomatoes. Season with salt and freshly ground black pepper. Sprinkle with the black olives and grated Romano cheese. Place the tomatoes under the broiler for 5 minutes, or until the cheese is melted and begins to brown. Remove from the broiler, garnish with the minced parsley and serve. Serves 4.

PAN-FRIED BREADED TOMATOES

4 medium, firm tomatoes
Salt
Fresh, finely ground black pepper
2 large eggs
2 tbsp. water
2 cups fine bread crumbs
½ cup butter
2 lemons, halved crosswise

Wash, stem, and slice the tomatoes crosswise into ½" thick rounds. Sprinkle one side lightly with salt and set aside in a single layer on a clean cloth to drain excess moisture for about 15 minutes. Turn the tomatoes over, salt lightly, and drain on the other side for another 15 minutes. Wipe the drained tomato rounds dry of moisture and season with the fresh, finely ground black pepper. In a small mixing bowl, beat the two eggs together with the water. Dredge the tomato rounds in bread crumbs, dip in the egg-wash, and dredge again in bread crumbs.

In a wide skillet or sauté pan, melt the butter and fry the bread crumb-coated tomato rounds quickly until lightly browned on both sides, turning only once during the cooking. Do not cook at so high a temperature that the butter burns. Transfer to plates and garnish with lemon halves. Serves 4.

Note: The bread crumbs are best if made from French bread, but any will do. Seasoned bread crumbs will add a good deal more flavor and zest to the recipe.

Try this as a bed for poached eggs, grilled fish fillets, or butter-sautéd shrimp, crayfish, lump crabmeat, or oysters.

Any oil of your preference—olive, peanut, corn, canola, safflower—can be used in place of the butter. In the old days, good beef lard would have been used to fry these tomatoes and the taste was quite delicious. Try using bacon drippings for the oil, if you have them handy.

FRIED TOMATOES IN CRACKER CRUMBS

4 medium unripe tomatoes
1 whole raw egg
½ cup milk
¼ tsp. cayenne pepper
1 cup rolled saltine cracker crumbs
Oil for frying
1 lemon, quartered

Cut the tomatoes in vertical rounds about ½" thick. Set aside. Beat the egg together with the milk and cayenne pepper. Dip the tomato rounds in the egg mixture and dredge in the cracker crumbs. Fry in the oil heated to 375 degrees for 5 minutes. Drain on absorbent paper. Serve with lemon wedges. Serves 4.

Note: Fried tomatoes are only good when they are hot so be sure that they are cooked at the very last minute.

You may want to sauté in butter with a little parsley added, as opposed to cooking in deep fat, and serve with the pan drippings poured over the tomatoes.

French bread crumbs with a little salt added, or seasoned Italian bread crumbs, can be used in place of the rolled cracker crumbs.

GRILLED TOMATO ROUNDS

4 medium-sized, slightly underripe tomatoes
Salt to taste
Black pepper, freshly ground, to taste

Slice the tomatoes into three rounds each, cutting off the stem top and an edge off the bottom to allow them to stand flat on the grill. Season with salt and freshly ground black pepper.

When you are ready to cook the tomato rounds, place them directly on the grill rack and close the cover. Let cook for 10-15 minutes, or until they are heated through, but have not begun to become soft, or begun to collapse. Do not flip the tomato rounds during the cooking: cook on the one side only.

When ready, carefully remove the cooked tomato slices from the grill with a spatula wide enough to lift the whole rounds without them hanging off the sides of the spatula—in which case they might break—and place directly on the dinner plates. They are delicate at this point and should not be handled more than necessary. Serves 4.

Note: Variations on this recipe would include a pinch of chopped fresh herbs such as basil, dill, oregano, or cilantro, sprinkled on the tomatoes before cooking.

The addition of grated Parmesan or Romano cheese also makes a fine recipe.

The simplest of grilled tomatoes are those sliced into rounds, simply seasoned, and placed on the grill until they are well heated, but not yet collapsing. The variations on this recipe are endless: whatever spice, herb, or cheese you choose to enhance the recipe can only make it better.

It is an especially convenient vegetable course to have when the grill is already in use for the entree. Simply place the tomato slices around the edges of the grill rack, around the chicken, fish, or whatever, and allow them to cook at the same time. The tomatoes will not take as long as some of your entrees, so you will want to place them on the grill some ten or fifteen minutes before the entree is done. It is the flavor from the grill smoke that really adds the nice touch to this preparation.

GRILL-ROASTED TOMATOES

4 medium tomatoes
Olive oil
Salt to taste
Black pepper, freshly ground, to taste

Brush the tomatoes with olive oil and place directly on the grill rack over hot coals. Turn the tomatoes until they are blackened and blistered on all sides. This will take approximately 10-15 minutes.

Remove the tomatoes from the grill and rub off the skin. Season with salt and freshly ground black pepper. Serves 4.

Note: These tomatoes can be eaten just as they are, or they can be added to other recipes such as salads, rice, or sauces.

GRILLED MARINATED TOMATOES

⅓ cup soy sauce
¼ cup balsamic vinegar
Salt to taste
1 tsp. hot sauce, or to taste
4 medium tomatoes
Black pepper, freshly ground, to taste

Make a marinade by combining the soy sauce with the balsamic vinegar, salt, and hot sauce. Stir until the salt is dissolved. Cut the tomatoes into three or four rounds each and marinate in the liquid ingredients for 30 minutes. Grill the marinated tomato rounds for seven minutes or so, depending on the heat of the grill apparatus, or until the tomatoes are cooked through, but not so well cooked that they begin to collapse. Remove from the grill, season lightly with salt and freshly ground black pepper, and serve. Serves 4.

WHOLE GRILLED TOMATOES

4 medium-sized, firm, ripe tomatoes,
   or 8-12 ripe Roma tomatoes
Olive oil
Salt to taste
Black pepper, freshly ground, to taste

Cut out the stems of the tomatoes in a circle large enough to insert a teaspoon. Use a teaspoon to scoop out the seeds; discard them. Brush the tomatoes with olive oil and sprinkle inside and out with salt and pepper. Place the prepared tomatoes on the hot rack of a charcoal grill, or under an oven broiler. Cook quickly, for about 5-7 minutes, turning once midway, or until the tomatoes are cooked but not so cooked that they begin to collapse. Serve. Serves 4.

Note: Another simple and extremely basic recipe is this one, which does offer an easy-to-prepare and readily available vegetable course to round out any meal.

Good tomatoes need very little to make them welcomed as part of a meal. In this recipe, any tomato can be used. If you choose to use Roma tomatoes over regular tomatoes, you should prepare and serve two to three per person, depending on the size of the Romas.

GRILLED ROMA TOMATOES WITH FRESH DILL

8 Roma tomatoes
½ tbsp. minced fresh dill
Salt to taste
Black pepper, freshly ground, to taste

Cut off the stem end of the tomatoes and slice them in half lengthwise. Lay them cut-side up on a plate and sprinkle them with the minced fresh dill. Season with salt and freshly ground black pepper.

On the hot rack of the heated grill, place the tomatoes, cut-side up, over the hot coals, cover, and cook for about 12 minutes, or until they are cooked but not collapsing. The texture of the tomatoes should still be firm enough that the tomatoes hold their shape, rather than sinking down into their skins.

When cooked, remove carefully with a spatula and handle as little as possible before serving. Serves 4.

Note: Roma tomatoes have a firm texture and sometimes work better than other available tomatoes in recipes where you need the stronger texture to hold the tomato together during the cooking.

The fact that I have used dill in this recipe is incidental. Your choice of fresh minced herbs will do equally as well. You may want to substitute fresh oregano, basil, mint, cilantro, thyme, or whatever you have available.

Grated Romano or Parmesan cheese added in place of, or in addition to, the herbs makes a fine tomato course.

STEWED TOMATOES

6 medium tomatoes
Boiling water
2 tbsp. butter
½ cup rolled cracker crumbs
1 tsp. sugar
Salt to taste
Black pepper, freshly ground, to taste

Pour boiling water over the tomatoes and allow let them to remain in it a few minutes to scald the skins. Remove the tomatoes from the water and skin them.

Cut the skinned tomatoes into quarters and put them in a saucepan with the butter, cracker crumbs, and sugar. Season with salt and freshly ground black pepper, cover, and simmer gently for 20 minutes. Serves 4.

STEWED OKRA AND TOMATOES

2 tbsp. butter
1 small onion, chopped
2 cups sliced okra
2 cloves garlic, chopped
2 large tomatoes, chopped
½ cup chicken stock
1 tbsp. vinegar
1 bay leaf
⅛ tsp. thyme
⅛ tsp. cayenne pepper
Salt to taste
Black pepper, freshly ground, to taste

In a heavy saucepan, melt the butter and sauté the onion, okra, and garlic. When they begin to color, add the tomatoes, chicken stock, vinegar, bay leaf, thyme, and cayenne pepper. Season to taste with salt and freshly ground black pepper. Simmer gently for 20 minutes, or until the ingredients have become a thick stew. Serves 4.

BRAZILIAN STEWED OKRA WITH TOMATOES

½ lb. fresh small tender okra
8 Roma tomatoes, stemmed and quartered lengthwise
1 medium onion, quartered and separated
1 cup water
2 tsp. minced fresh sweet basil
1 tsp. minced habanero chili pepper
Salt to taste

Wash the okra and slice off and discard the stem ends and the tip ends. The liquids should be able to pass through the okra pods, one end to the other, during the cooking.

In a saucepan, combine the okra, the Roma tomatoes, onion, water, and sweet basil. Place the saucepan on the heat and add the habanero pepper and season to taste with salt. Simmer for about 20 minutes, or until the okra are tender. Check seasonings before serving. Serves 4.

Note: The juices released from the okra in the cooking will bring a rich and syrupy consistency to the cooking liquids in the pot. A splash of red wine vinegar to finish the dish would add a nice subtle bite to the flavors here. If you prefer, you can cut the okra pods crosswise into ½" thick rounds.

Tomatoes show up stewed with just about every imaginable vegetable. Okra and tomatoes is a dish that is common in the areas of the world where the cuisine might be referred to as Creole.

STEAMED TOMATOES

4 medium tomatoes
Water
Salt and freshly ground black pepper
¼ cup hot melted butter
Juice from 1 lemon

Wash the tomatoes and cut the stems off. Place them in a colander over a pot filled with steaming water. Steam for 15 minutes or until the tomatoes are tender. Rub off the skins. Season with salt and freshly ground black pepper and reheat. Combine the melted butter and lemon juice and pour it over the tomatoes. Serves 4.

Note: A teaspoon of chopped garlic or parsley added to the melted butter will enhance the recipe.

ROASTED TOMATOES

4 large tomatoes
Salt to taste
Black pepper, freshly ground, to taste

Line a baking pan with foil. Place the tomatoes on the pan and under a broiler, close as possible to the flame, and let them roast on one side until the skin is black and blistered. Turn and repeat process on the other side. This will take approximately 15 minutes or less, depending on your broiler. Remove from the heat and hold under running water to rub off the skin. To serve, season with salt and freshly ground black pepper and heat. Serves 4.

CHINESE STIR-FRIED TOMATOES IN EGG SAUCE

2 medium raw eggs
3 tbsp. peanut oil
½ tsp. salt
2 cloves garlic, minced
2 green onions, minced
1 tbsp. sherry
5 medium tomatoes, skinned, seeded,
    and sliced into six wedges each
¼ tsp. ground white pepper
1 tbsp. sugar
1 tsp. chicken stock base, or mashed bouillon cube
    or powder
1 tbsp. cornstarch mixed with 1½ tbsp. *cold* water
1 tsp. sesame oil

In a small bowl, beat the eggs with 1 tbsp. peanut oil and a pinch of the salt. Hold aside.

Heat a wok or deep sauté pan very hot and add the remaining peanut oil. Add the garlic and green onions and stir-fry briefly. Add the sherry carefully and then the tomatoes, stir-frying for a minute only. Season the tomatoes with salt, white pepper, sugar, and stock base or bouillon base and stir all together well.

Press the tomatoes to the sides of the wok or sauté pan and allow the juices to collect in the middle. Stir in the cornstarch and water and allow to thicken. Stir the tomatoes back down into the thickened liquids. Pour the egg mixture in a thin stream around and over the tomatoes, stir them in to cook. Stir in the sesame oil to flavor the dish and serve. Serves 4.

TOMATO RICE

2 cups tomato pulp, finely chopped
1 tbsp. butter
1 medium onion, finely chopped
½ cup water
¼ tsp. powdered marjoram
1½ tsp. salt
¼ tsp. ground white pepper
1½ cups uncooked white rice

Pass the tomato pulp through a strainer and hold aside.

In a saucepan, heat the butter and sauté the chopped onion until it begins to color. Add the water, tomato pulp, marjoram, salt, and pepper. Bring to a boil, add the rice, cover, and cook at a simmer for 20 minutes, or until rice is cooked and all the liquids are absorbed. Serves 4-6.

TOMATO GRITS

1 strip bacon
$2\frac{2}{3}$ cups beef stock, chicken stock, or water
$\frac{2}{3}$ cup grits
2 medium tomatoes, chopped
2 tbsp. Tomato Paste
1 green onion, chopped
1 small clove garlic, minced
$\frac{1}{2}$ cup grated cheddar cheese
$\frac{1}{2}$ tsp. salt
Louisiana hot sauce, optional

Finely chop the bacon and add it to a saucepan to heat. When the fat is rendered and the bacon is cooked, add the beef, chicken stock, or water, and bring to a boil. Add the grits, tomatoes, Tomato Paste, green onion, garlic, cheddar cheese, salt, and a dash of Louisiana hot sauce, if so desired. Bring to a boil, cover, and turn down to a simmer. Cook for 20 minutes or until the grits are tender and thick. Remove from the heat and let sit for a minute or so until thickened to desired consistency. Serves 4.

Note: The cheddar cheese can be substituted with something more tantalizing like Camembert or Roquefort, or something simpler like American white or farmer cheese. Try it with goat cheese and add some fresh chopped herbs to suit your taste.

Grits is an American tradition because it was first used here by the native peoples. These peoples, incorrectly dubbed "Indians" by Columbus, relied on corn in its many forms—grits being a most important form—as their base of cooking.

The Europeans who settled the southern areas of what is now the United States were heavily reliant on the kindness and generosity of the native Indians for foodstuffs and for education in the ways of hunting and the farming of indigenous vegetation for food crops. Corn and grits were the most important of all cultivated foods and remain today a most important element in American cookery, especially Southern cooking.

BAKED TOMATO AND CORN CASSEROLE

4 tbsp. butter
1½ cups stewed tomatoes
1½ cups cooked corn kernels
1 small sweet green pepper, stemmed, seeded,
  and chopped
1 medium onion, thinly sliced
1 green onion, chopped
1 tbsp. chopped parsley
⅛ tsp. ground allspice
Salt to taste
Black pepper, freshly ground, to taste
1 cup dry bread crumbs
¼ cup grated Parmesan cheese

Preheat the oven to 400 degrees.

In a saucepan or covered skillet, melt 2 tbsp. butter and cook the stewed tomatoes, corn, green pepper, onion, green onion, parsley, and allspice together over a medium-low heat for about 15 minutes. Season to taste with salt and freshly ground black pepper.

Butter a baking dish and sprinkle in a thin layer of bread crumbs. Continue with a layer of the cooked vegetables, then bread crumbs, then vegetables, and finish with a final layer of bread crumbs. Sprinkle the grated Parmesan cheese over the top, dot with the remaining 2 tbsp. butter, and bake in the 400-degree oven for 10 minutes, or until the top crust is nicely browned and most of the liquids are absorbed. Serves 4-6.

AVIGNON TOMATO
AND EGGPLANT CASSEROLE

1 large eggplant
Salt
½ cup flour
¼ cup olive oil
4 medium-sized tomatoes, skinned, seeded,
**   and diced**
2 cloves garlic, minced
½ tsp. sugar
½ cup bread crumbs
Black pepper, freshly ground, to taste
¼ cup grated Parmesan cheese
1½ tbsp. melted butter

Preheat the oven to 375 degrees.

Remove the stem and skin of the eggplant, and cut it crosswise into ½" thick slices. Lay the round slices in a single layer on a plate, sprinkle liberally with salt, and set aside for about 30 minutes to allow the salt to draw the excess moisture from the eggplant rounds. Wipe the salt and moisture from the eggplant rounds, and dredge them in flour.

In a wide skillet, heat all but 1 tbsp. olive oil and fry the eggplant rounds, turning once, until browned on both sides. Remove from the heat.

In the same skillet, heat the remaining 1 tbsp. olive oil and add the tomatoes, garlic, and sugar. Cook for approximately 5 minutes, only long enough to render and reduce the tomato liquids somewhat. Add 1 tbsp. bread crumbs and season to taste with salt and freshly ground black pepper.

In a casserole or baking dish, arrange the eggplant rounds and tomatoes in layers beginning with eggplant on the bottom and ending with tomatoes as the top layer.

Combine the remaining bread crumbs with the grated Parmesan cheese and sprinkle over the top. Dribble the melted butter over the casserole.

Bake for 30 minutes, or until the bread crumb and cheese top, or "gratin," is browned. Serves 4.

SCALLOPED TOMATOES AND ONIONS

3 small onions, skinned
3 cups Stewed Tomatoes
2 tsp. brown sugar
⅛ tsp. ground allspice
¾ cup bread crumbs
Salt to taste
Black pepper, freshly ground, to taste
2 tbsp. butter

Preheat the oven to 350 degrees.

In a pot, bring enough water to cover the onions to a boil and add the skinned onions. Boil for 5 minutes and remove to drain and cool enough to handle. Slice the parboiled onions crosswise into thin slices.

In a bowl, fold the Stewed Tomatoes together with the brown sugar and ground allspice.

In a buttered baking dish, or pie pan, begin the layering of ingredients with bread crumbs, then tomatoes, then onions; then repeat with layers of bread crumbs, tomatoes, and onions; finish off with an additional top layer of bread crumbs. Season the layers lightly with salt and pepper as you go.

Dot the top bread crumb layer with butter and bake for about 20 minutes or until the top crust is nicely browned and the liquids are absorbed. Serves 4.

KENYAN COLLARDS WITH TOMATOES AND COCONUT MILK

1 lb. collard greens, washed and rough-chopped
1 red onion, chopped
1 cup coconut milk
½ cup chicken stock or water
3 tomatoes, diced
Salt to taste
Cayenne pepper to taste

In a pot, combine the prepared collard greens with the chopped red onion, coconut milk, and chicken stock or water. Cover and simmer for 20 minutes. Add the tomatoes, return to a boil, and season to taste with salt and cayenne pepper. Cook, uncovered, for 10 more minutes or until most of the liquid is reduced. Serves 4.

Note: Mustard greens can be used here as well as the collard greens. Spinach can also be used, provided you reduce the greens' cooking time by half.

TOMATOES MIREILLE

1 medium-sized eggplant
Salt to taste
⅓ cup light olive oil or peanut oil
4 large tomatoes, skinned, quartered, and seeded
2 large cloves garlic, chopped
2 tbsp. chopped parsley
1 tbsp. chopped fresh basil or 1 tsp. dried basil
½ tsp. sugar
Black pepper, freshly ground, to taste
½ cup flour

Peel the eggplant and cut it crosswise into ¼" round slices. Place the eggplant rounds on a platter in a single layer and salt them. Set them aside for 30 minutes or so to give the salt time to draw the excess moisture from the eggplant slices.

Heat 1 tbsp. olive oil in a sauté pan and add the tomato quarters. Add the garlic, 1½ tbsp. parsley, the basil, and sugar and stir all together well. Season to taste with salt and freshly ground black pepper. Cook for only about 5 minutes, or until the excess moisture from the tomatoes is almost completely reduced. Hold aside warm.

THE TOMATO COOKBOOK

Take the eggplant rounds, wipe them dry, and dredge them in the flour. In a skillet, heat the remaining olive oil and sauté the eggplant rounds, until browned on both sides. Turn them only once during the cooking and handle them as little as possible. They may become fragile. Remove the cooked rounds to four vegetable plates, arranging them in a circle with their edges overlapping, and spoon the cooked seasoned, tomatoes onto the center of each serving. Garnish with the remaining ½ tbsp. chopped parsley. Serves 4.

Note: Again in this dish we see the southern French influence, a definite Mediterranean influence. Although I have included several recipes that employ the marriage of tomatoes with eggplant, they are each quite different in their presentation.

TOMATOES PORTUGUESE

2 tbsp. olive oil
4 medium whole tomatoes, skinned and seeded
4 green onions, chopped
2 large cloves garlic, chopped
½ tsp. brown sugar
½ cup bread crumbs
Salt to taste
Black pepper, freshly ground, to taste
1 tbsp. chopped parsley

In a skillet or sauté pan, heat the olive oil and sauté the tomatoes for about 5 minutes, or until they begin to lose their shape.

Add the green onions, garlic, and brown sugar. Cook for 1 minute together, then add the bread crumbs. Season to taste with salt and freshly ground black pepper. Continue heating until all is good and hot. Transfer to a serving dish. Garnish with the chopped parsley. Serves 4.

Note: I always use French bread crumbs, but whatever you may have available will do. If you make your own from stale bread, be sure that the bread is dry so they will absorb the cooking juices.

The Portuguese were one of the first European peoples to utilize the New World tomatoes in their cooking.

CHILI TOMATO RICE WITH PETITS POIS

1 10-oz. can Rotel diced tomatoes with green chilies
1 15-oz. can tomato puree, no salt added
1 cup finely chopped onion
½ cup water
2 tbsp. olive oil
½ tsp. dried basil
½ tsp. salt
¼ tsp. freshly ground black pepper
1 10-oz. packet Vigo Preseasoned Yellow Rice
   (Arroz Amarillo)
1 16-oz. can fine petits pois (young green peas)

In a saucepan, combine the Rotel diced tomatoes with green chilies, tomato puree, onion, water, olive oil, basil, salt, and pepper. Bring to a boil. Add the contents of the packet of the Vigo Preseasoned Yellow Rice and return to a boil. Stir all together well, cover, and turn down to a simmer. Simmer for 25 minutes, or until all the liquid is absorbed and the rice is cooked.

When the rice is about to be served, fluff it up with a wooden spoon. Drain the water from the peas and add them to the rice. Be careful not to mash them in the process. Adjust seasonings if necessary. Continue to heat only long enough to allow the contents of the saucepan to become good and hot. Serve. Serves 6 amply.

Note: This recipe will result in a rice that holds together, rather than one where the rice remains perfectly separate, one grain from the other. I generally use long grain rice, any number of brands, but I do not use converted rice (and never instant rice), which to me seems less tasty and somewhat plastic, if I may use that word. The concept that rice should always be perfectly individually separate after cooking, and does not stick together, is one that does not work well with many Louisiana dishes, or the rice dishes of most countries.

This dish can be spooned out or even packed into a coffee cup to form it into a neat mound. It will hold that shape.

Using canned products in cooking has not been a normal procedure for me in the past. It happens, though, that some of the rare canned products that I do find acceptable are tomato products and petits pois, both of which are employed here.

The Rotel tomatoes with green chilies will add a heat that is tasty without being excessive.

This recipe also employs a preseasoned yellow rice that adds a nice touch of seasoning without having to add much more. White or brown rice could certainly be used in the place of the preseasoned yellow rice, while you might need a bit more salt and pepper. All make a quite satisfactory rice dish.

UGANDAN SAUTEED MIXED VEGETABLES

¼ **cup peanut oil**
1 small onion, chopped
1 small eggplant, skinned and diced
1 small sweet green pepper, julienned
4 cloves garlic, pressed
1 lb. fresh spinach, washed and rough-chopped
1 small zucchini, diced
4 medium tomatoes, rough-chopped
Salt to taste
Black pepper, freshly ground, to taste

In a wide skillet or sauté pan, heat the peanut oil and sauté the onions, eggplant, and green pepper together for 2 minutes. Add the garlic, spinach, and zucchini. Cover and simmer for 10 minutes. Add the tomatoes, cover, and simmer for 15 more minutes, or until all vegetables are tender and cooked completely. Season to taste with salt and freshly ground black pepper. Serves 4.

Aside from the great variety and ingenuity that went into the creation of these recipes, they are inexpensive to prepare. But don't let yourself be deceived by the economical nature of the dishes themselves. They make as delicious a meal as any of the more expensive meals here.

AFRICAN TOMATO AND POTATO CURRY

¼ cup peanut oil
1 large onion, chopped
4 cloves garlic, chopped
2 medium potatoes, diced
1 tsp. fresh grated ginger
1 tsp. cumin
1 tsp. cardamom
½ tsp. cinnamon
1 tsp. turmeric
½ tsp. cayenne pepper
¾ cup (6 oz.) Tomato Paste
4 large tomatoes, cut into large dice
½ cup chopped fresh cilantro
3 cups hot cooked brown rice

In a saucepan, heat the peanut oil and fry the chopped onion and garlic until they begin to color. Add the potatoes, ginger, cumin, cardamom, cinnamon, turmeric, cayenne pepper, and Tomato Paste. Cook together for 5 minutes. Add the tomatoes, cover, and simmer for 10 minutes. Fold in the cilantro and serve over hot brown rice. Serves 4.

CHINESE STIR-FRIED CABBAGE WITH TOMATO

1 1-lb. head cabbage
3 tbsp. peanut oil
2 cloves garlic, minced
4 medium tomatoes, skinned, seeded,
   and cut into thin wedges
1 tsp. salt
1 tsp. sugar
⅛ tsp. ground white pepper

Prep the cabbage, cutting the leaves into pieces measuring one by two inches.

Heat a wok or deep sauté pan and add the oil. Stir-fry the garlic until lightly browned and then add the cabbage. Stir-fry the cabbage for about 4 minutes or until the cabbage is limp. Add the tomato wedges, salt, sugar, and pepper and continue stir-frying for about 2 minutes more. Remove from heat, cover, and let stand for 2 minutes. Stir up the ingredients and serve. Serves 4.

CARIBBEAN BLACK BEANS AND TOMATOES

1 cup black beans
1 qt. boiling water
4 cups water
½ cup diced salt pork
1 cup chopped onions
3 cups chopped tomatoes
3 clover minced garlic cloves
4 bay leaves
⅛ tsp. cayenne pepper
1 tsp. turmeric
⅛ tsp. allspice
1 tbsp. vinegar
Salt to taste
Black pepper, freshly ground, to taste

Cover beans with boiling water and soak overnight.

In a bean pot, heat and fry the diced salt pork until the fat is rendered and the dice are crisp. Remove the pieces from the pot with a slotted spoon to leave all the fat. Add the onions and garlic and brown. Add remaining ingredients and seasonings. Simmer for 2 hours or until the beans are of a desired tenderness and the liquids have thickened. Serves 4.

Note: Pigeon peas can also be used in this recipe.

WHITE BEANS WITH TOMATOES AND TOMATO RICE

1 cup Great Northern white beans
1½ qt. water or stock
1 medium onion, chopped
4 green onions, chopped
¼ bunch parsley, stems and leaves, chopped
1 rib celery, chopped
2 large cloves garlic, chopped
2 bay leaves
½ cup white wine
¼ cup cream sherry
1 tbsp. vinegar
1 tsp. cane syrup
½ tsp. curry powder
1 tsp. chili powder
¼ tsp. dried thyme
¼ tsp. dried oregano
¼ tsp. dried tarragon
¼ tsp. dried basil
Salt to taste
Black pepper, freshly ground, to taste
4 medium tomatoes, chopped
2 tbsp. Tomato Paste
1 tsp. habanero pepper sauce, or Louisiana hot sauce
3 cups hot Tomato Rice, or fluffy cooked white rice

Rinse and pick over the beans to be sure there is no dust or pebbles in the package. Put the beans in a saucepan with the water, cover, and let them soak overnight.

In the morning, add all the remaining ingredients (except for the Tomato Rice) to the pot with the beans. Put the pot on to heat, bring to a boil, turn down to the merest of simmers, cover, and cook for 1½ hours, or until the beans are quite tender. If the beans become too dry before they are properly cooked, add water, a cup at a time. When the beans are cooked, you can thicken the liquids in the pot by mashing some of the cooked beans against the inside of the pot with a wooden spoon. This makes a nice "gravy" for the beans and for the rice. Adjust seasonings.

To serve, spoon out the Tomato Rice, or white rice, onto plates or into large soup bowls and ladle the beans over the rice. Serve additional hot sauce and/or pickled hot peppers on the table with the beans. Serves 4.

Note: The soaking of the beans allows them to begin rehydrating gradually rather than too quickly during cooking, in which case the skins might burst from the beans: it is not a necessary step. If you don't soak the beans, be sure to cook them at a very low simmer for at least 3 hours.

MACARONI NEAPOLITAN

2 tbsp. butter
2 tbsp. light olive oil
1 medium onion, minced
1 lb. skinned, seeded, and chopped tomatoes
1 tbsp. minced fresh sweet basil leaves
Salt to taste
Black pepper, freshly ground, to taste
1 lb. long macaroni
4 tbsp. butter
2 cups grated Parmesano Reggiano

In a sauté pan, heat the butter and olive oil and sauté the minced onion until the mass browns lightly.

Add the tomatoes and sweet basil leaves. Season to taste with salt, bearing in mind that the salty Parmesano Reggiano will be added later, and freshly ground black pepper. Simmer gently, uncovered for 45 minutes.

Cook the long macaroni according to package directions, drain out the cooking water, and rinse the cooked macaroni with fresh water. In the pot in which you cooked the macaroni, combine the rinsed cooked macaroni with the butter, the cooked tomato sauce, and 1 cup of the grated Parmesano Reggiano. Heat it well and serve it up with the remaining Parmesano Reggiano in a bowl and a peppermill at the table. Serves 4.

Note: Carefully conserve all liquids rendered in the preparation of the tomatoes for cooking and add it to the sauce with the chopped tomatoes.

EGGS

There was a time before mass production when the egg was considered far more of a delicacy than it is today. Many elegant recipes exist that make the best use of its unique and variable qualities.

Although Americans tend to consider the egg as a breakfast item more than as anything else, most other countries still consider the egg to be an important and marvelous food.

These egg dishes give a sampling of some of those elegant recipes.

BAKED EGGS IN TOMATOES

4 medium tomatoes
Salt
4 large raw eggs
Black pepper, freshly ground, to taste
4 tsp. butter

Preheat oven to 450 degrees.

Slice off the stem end of the tomatoes and scoop out their insides. Use the removed tomato for other recipes. Sprinkle the interior walls of the tomato shells with salt and place them upside down in a baking dish. Place the dish in the oven for 5 minutes.

Remove the inverted tomatoes from the oven, pour off the pan liquids, and set them upright in the baking dish.

Break a raw egg into each tomato and season with salt and freshly ground black pepper. Place 1 tsp. butter on the egg in each tomato. Return the tomatoes to the oven and bake for 5 minutes, or until the whites are cooked firm, but the yolk is not. Serve immediately. Serves 4.

FRIED EGGS MIREILLE

4 tbsp. butter
8 chicken livers, diced
Salt to taste
Black pepper, freshly ground, to taste
4 medium-sized tomatoes, washed and stemmed
8 fried eggs
1 cup Madeira Sauce

In a small sauté pan, heat 2 tbsp. of the butter, briefly sauté the diced chicken livers, and season them with salt and freshly ground black pepper. Hold aside warm.

Slice the tomatoes crosswise into ½" rounds. In a wide skillet, heat the remaining 2 tbsp. butter and sauté the tomatoes, turning once, and seasoning them during the cooking with salt and freshly ground black pepper.

To serve, arrange the tomato slices on four plates and lay two fried eggs on each serving. Garnish with the chicken livers and spoon the Madeira Sauce over each dish. Serves 4.

Note: There are several recipes in this collection that include the name Mireille. They all differ somewhat, depending on with what food the *mireille*—garnish or preparation—is to be served. This particular preparation is very fine with its use of the Madeira Sauce.

FRIED EGGS MISTRAL

4 tbsp. butter
4 medium-sized tomatoes, halved
1 dozen good quality olives, black or green,
   halved and pitted
Salt to taste
Black pepper, freshly ground, to taste
8 fried eggs

In a skillet, heat the butter and sauté the tomatoes with the olives for about 4 minutes, turning once, until the tomatoes are cooked but still holding their shape fairly well. Season with salt and freshly ground black pepper.

Place two cooked tomato halves, cut-side up, in the center of each of four plates, two eggs, one on each side of the centered tomato halves, and strew the olive halves over the eggs. Serves 4.

Note: Le Mistral is the name that the French have given to the strong wind that blows across France from the north to the south.

There is another Mistral in France and that is the express train, the *TGV*, as they call it, initials for the French words meaning the "train of great speed." The Mistral leaves Paris in the evening and arrives near the shores of the Mediterranean (across the country) in the morning of the following day.

EGG AND TOMATO SANDWICH

8 Roma tomatoes, stemmed
8 hard-boiled eggs
2 green onions, chopped
Tomato Mayonnaise
8 slices of toast or toasted French bread
4 leaves lettuce, washed
1 small red onion, sliced paper-thin
Salt to taste
Black pepper, freshly ground, to taste

Choose tomatoes that are not much wider than an egg. Slice the tomatoes crosswise into ¼" thick slices.

Slice the hard-boiled eggs crosswise into ¼" thick rounds.

Fold the green onions into the Tomato Mayonnaise and spread each piece of toast or toasted French bread with the onion-mayonnaise mixture.

Lay a leaf of lettuce on a half of each sandwich and top with alternating layers of sliced tomatoes, red onions, and hard-boiled egg. Season lightly with salt and freshly ground black pepper. Serves 4.

Note: Try Russian Tomato Dressing here as the sandwich spread.

PORTUGUESE SCRAMBLED EGGS

2 tbsp. butter
4 medium-sized tomatoes, skinned, seeded,
  and chopped
8 large eggs
⅓ cup light cream
Salt to taste
Black pepper, freshly ground, to taste
Dash Louisiana hot sauce
2 tbsp. minced parsley

In a skillet, melt the butter and sauté the tomatoes until most of the liquid is evaporated.

In a bowl, beat the eggs together with the light cream. Pour the egg mixture into the skillet with the cooked tomatoes. Stir together to scramble the mixture while cooking. Season with salt and freshly ground black pepper, add a dash of Louisiana hot sauce, and add the minced parsley. Serves 4.

Note: The Portuguese people were among the first Europeans to adopt the newly "discovered" tomato from the New World.

Before these contemporary times of swift transportation and refrigeration, the egg historically played a far more important role in world cuisines than it does now. It was natural for the Portuguese to join the egg with the tomato early on in their experimentation with the new fruit, as the tomato is in actuality a fruit and not a vegetable.

HUEVOS RANCHEROS

¼ cup lard or oil
4 corn tortillas, store-bought or your own recipe
8 large eggs
Salt to taste
Black pepper, freshly ground, to taste
2 cups Tomato and Chili Sauce
2 tbsp. mild goat cheese or feta, crumbled

In a wide skillet, heat the lard or oil and quickly fry the corn tortillas for a few seconds on each side, one at a time. Drain the tortillas on absorbent paper and place them on four plates. Hold warm in the oven.

Fry the eggs in the remaining fat and, using a spatula, transfer them two at a time onto the four warming tortillas. Season with salt and pepper. Spoon the Tomato and Chili Sauce over the eggs and sprinkle with crumbled goat or feta cheese. Serves 4.

TOMATO SOUFFLE CASSEROLE

2 tbsp. butter
2 tbsp. flour
¾ cup scalded milk
3 cups fresh tomato puree
Pinch nutmeg
Pinch cayenne pepper
1 tsp. salt
¼ tsp. white pepper
2 large eggs, separated

Preheat the oven to 350 degrees.

In a saucepan, melt the butter and blend in the flour. Let cook together for 2 minutes, allowing it to foam up in the process. Gradually whisk in the hot scalded milk and bring to a boil. Cook until the sauce is thickened somewhat. Add the tomato puree, nutmeg, cayenne pepper, salt, and white pepper. Simmer gently for 15 minutes. Remove from heat to cool.

Beat the egg yolks until thick and pale yellow and fold into the cooled soufflé base. Beat the egg whites to the soft-peak stage and fold by thirds into the soufflé base. Transfer the mixture into a buttered soufflé casserole or deep baking dish and bake in the preheated oven for 30 minutes, or until the soufflé has risen and browned on top. Serve immediately. Serves 4.

SEAFOOD

When you consider the miles of the earth's land mass that are bordered by the sea, or that contain lakes and rivers from which so many of the finest fish and seafood are taken, you would have to understand the vast array of tomato-based seafood dishes that exist.

As with poultry and all other principal food products, the tomato and the fish make a perfect marriage.

Some of the recipes here are familiar favorites; others are more obscure. But, nonetheless, they are all delicious.

TOMATO FISH RAGOUT

4 tbsp. butter
4 tbsp. flour
½ cup minced green onions
¼ cup minced sweet green pepper
1½ cups chopped tomato pulp
1 cup scalded milk
1½ lb. raw fresh fish fillet, diced
⅛ tsp. ground nutmeg
Salt to taste
White pepper to taste
8 toasted, buttered French bread croutons

In a saucepan, melt the butter and stir in the flour. Stir and let foam for 2 minutes. Add the green onions and green pepper and sauté for a minute more. Add the tomato pulp and the scalded milk. Simmer for 20 minutes, or until thickened. Add the diced fish fillet and the nutmeg. Season to taste with salt and white pepper. Serve over buttered French bread croutons. Serves 4.

Note: Simplicity is the key here. Ripe tomatoes and fresh fish are what make the recipe.

SHRIMP CREOLE

4 tbsp. butter
3 large onions, rough-chopped
2 large bell peppers, seeded and rough-chopped
1 stalk celery, minced
4 cloves garlic, minced
5 large tomatoes, skinned, seeded, and rough-chopped
1 tsp. thyme
4 bay leaves
1 tsp. paprika
2 tbsp. minced parsley
Salt to taste
White pepper to taste
¼ tsp. cayenne pepper, or to taste
1 tsp. cornstarch mixed with 1 tbsp. *cold* water
3 lb. whole raw shrimp, headed, peeled,
    and deveined
4 cups hot cooked rice

In a wide heavy skillet, melt the butter and sauté the onions, bell pepper, celery, and garlic until all becomes limp, about 3-5 minutes. Add the tomatoes, thyme, bay leaves, paprika, parsley, salt, pepper, and cayenne pepper. Simmer together for 10 minutes. Blend the cornstarch and water into the sauce. Bring to a simmer and cook for 2 minutes then add the shrimp. Let the shrimp remain in the sauce for just 3-5 minutes, or until they are cooked but not overcooked. Spoon the Shrimp Creole onto plates and top with a scoop of rice. Serves 6.

Note: The sauce of this dish is the essence of Creole cookery, and one that is influenced, among others, by both the Basque region of France and by Spain.

CRAYFISH CREOLE

4 tbsp. butter
2 medium onions, rough-chopped
1 large bell pepper, seeded and rough-chopped
1 stalk celery, minced
3 cloves garlic, minced
4 large tomatoes, skinned, seeded, and rough-chopped
½ tsp. thyme
2 bay leaves
1 tsp. paprika
2 tbsp. minced parsley
Salt to taste
White pepper to taste
¼ tsp. cayenne pepper, or to taste
1 tsp. cornstarch mixed with 1 tbsp. *cold* water
1 lb. crayfish tails
3 cups hot cooked rice

In a wide heavy skillet, melt the butter and sauté the onions, bell pepper, celery, and garlic until all becomes limp, about 5 minutes. Add the tomatoes, thyme, bay leaves, paprika, parsley, salt, pepper, and cayenne pepper. Simmer together for 10 minutes. Blend the cornstarch and water into the sauce. Bring to a simmer and cook for 2 minutes then add the crayfish tails. Let the crayfish tails remain in the sauce for just 3 minutes, or until they are cooked but not overcooked. Spoon the Crayfish Creole onto plates and top with a scoop of rice. Serves 4.

FISH FILLETS SIMMERED IN TOMATO AND LEEK SAUCE

½ cup butter
2 leeks, white part only, chopped
4 medium tomatoes, skinned, seeded, and chopped
1 clove garlic, minced
¼ tsp. oregano
¼ tsp. thyme
¼ tsp. paprika
½ cup dry white wine
1 cup Fish Stock
1 cup heavy cream
Salt to taste
White pepper to taste
Cayenne pepper to taste
4 6-oz. fresh fish fillets
2 tbsp. butter
1 dozen medium mushroom caps

In a saucepan, combine the butter, leeks, tomatoes, and seasonings with the white wine and Fish Stock. Bring to a boil and reduce to half. Add the heavy cream and reduce until the sauce has reached a relatively thick consistency. Season to taste with salt, white pepper, and cayenne pepper.

Pour the sauce into a wide sauté pan and lay in the fish fillets. Cover and simmer gently for 10 minutes, or until the fish fillets are completely cooked. While simmering the fish, heat in a second sauté pan 2 tbsp. butter and quickly sauté the mushroom caps. Keep warm. When the fish are cooked, carefully lift the fillets onto warmed dishes, spoon the sauce over each, and top with the sautéed mushroom caps. Serves 4.

GRILLED FISH FILLETS ANDALOUSE

2 tbsp. olive oil
2 large cloves garlic, chopped
1 large onion, chopped
1 medium bell pepper, seeded and chopped
1 small eggplant, cut into ½" dice
½ cup dry white wine
½ tsp. dried thyme
Salt to taste
White pepper, freshly ground, to taste
Cayenne pepper, to taste
4 medium tomatoes, skinned, seeded, and chopped
1½ tbsp. chopped parsley
4 6-oz. fresh fish fillets, including skin
2 tbsp. melted butter

In a sauté pan, heat the olive oil and sauté the garlic until lightly browned. Add the onion and bell pepper, and sauté for 10 minutes. Add the eggplant, white wine, and thyme; season with salt, pepper, and cayenne pepper; cover; and simmer for 15 minutes. Stir occasionally to prevent sticking and ensure even cooking. Add the tomatoes and chopped parsley, adjust seasonings, and heat only long enough for all to be hot. Brush the fish fillets with butter and season lightly with salt and pepper. Grill for 4 minutes on each side, or to desired doneness. Spoon the Andalouse vegetable mixture onto warm plates and place a grilled fillet of fish in the center of each. Garnish with more chopped parsley. Serves 4.

REDFISH COURT BOUILLON

½ cup butter
4 tbsp. flour
1 large onion, chopped
2 ribs celery, chopped
1 bunch green onions, chopped
2 cloves garlic, minced
3 large tomatoes, chopped
2 cups water or Fish Stock
½ cup red wine
1 tbsp. lemon juice
½ tsp. thyme
½ tsp. marjoram
3 bay leaves
¼ tsp. ground allspice
2 tbsp. salt
1 tsp. black pepper
½ tsp. cayenne pepper
4 8-oz. redfish fillets, or 1 3-4 lb. redfish,
    drawn and scaled.

Preheat the oven to 350 degrees.

Melt the butter in a wide, deep saucepan and add the flour. Cook together until the flour in the roux becomes light brown in color. Add the onions, celery, green onions, and garlic and continue cooking until the onions are limp. This should only take about 5 minutes. Add the tomatoes, water or stock, the wine, lemon juice, and all the seasoning spices and herbs. Simmer together for 15 minutes or so. Lay the redfish fillets, or whole redfish, into the sauce and baste with some of the sauce. Cover the pan and place in the oven for 20 minutes for the fillets or approximately 45 minutes for the whole fish, or until the flesh of the fish flakes when pierced with a fork. Baste several times during cooking. Serve with the sauce. Serves 4.

Note: The redfish is the fish that traditionally is used in this preparation, although any good fleshy fish can be used in this preparation. A whole fish, scaled and drawn, makes a marvelous presentation, although fish fillets taste just as good.

POACHED RED SNAPPER WITH AURORA SAUCE

AURORA SAUCE

3 tbsp. butter
2 tbsp. flour
1 cup hot Fish Stock
¾ cup tomato puree or Tomato Sauce
Salt to taste
White pepper, freshly ground, to taste
Cayenne pepper to taste

In a small saucepan, melt the butter and stir in the flour. Stir and cook until the mixture becomes foamy, about 2 minutes. Whisk in the hot stock and bring to a boil. Add the tomato puree or Tomato Sauce and season to taste with salt, white pepper, and cayenne pepper. Simmer for 15 minutes.

POACHING LIQUOR

Water
1 medium onion, sliced
1 lemon, sliced
4 bay leaves
8 whole peppercorns
4 whole allspice
2 tbsp. salt
½ tsp. cayenne pepper
1 3-lb. red snapper, drawn and scaled

In a large pan, add enough water to give you a 4" depth. Add the onion, lemon, bay leaves, peppercorns, allspice, salt, and cayenne pepper. Bring to a rolling boil for 5 minutes. Lay the fish into the seasoned water and cook at a gentle simmer for 15 minutes, or until the flesh of the fish is white and flaky all the way through. Carefully remove the fish from the water, drain, and place on a warmed serving platter. Spoon over it the Aurora Sauce. Serves 4.

AFRICAN SEAFOOD STEW

4 medium tomatoes
1 lb. skinned, boneless fresh fish fillets
1 lb. small raw shrimp with their heads still attached
1 qt. Fish Stock
2 tbsp. palm kernel oil or peanut oil
2 yellow onions, chopped
2 sweet green or red bell peppers, seeded and chopped
2 hot dried small red chili peppers, chopped
4 large cloves garlic, minced
¼ cup chopped fresh cilantro
2 tbsp. chopped fresh parsley
2 bay leaves
½ tsp. dried thyme
1 cup white wine
1 12-14 oz. can coconut milk
Salt to taste
Black pepper, freshly ground, to taste
1 tbsp. freshly squeezed lemon juice.

Skin, seed, and chop the tomatoes, reserving all the jelly and juices, and hold aside.

Cut the fish fillets into bite-sized pieces. Hold aside. Peel, head, and devein the shrimp and hold them aside. Put the heads and shells in a saucepan with the Fish Stock and bring to a boil. Boil gently for 10 minutes to render the juices and fat from the shrimp shells and heads. Strain the stock and discard the shells and heads.

In a soup pot, heat the oil and sauté the onions, bell peppers, chili peppers, and garlic until they begin to color. Add the prepared tomatoes, cilantro, parsley, bay leaves, and thyme. Now add the Fish Stock, white wine, and coconut milk and bring to a boil. Turn down to a simmer and cook for 20 minutes. Season to taste with salt and freshly ground black pepper. Only minutes before serving, add the fish fillet pieces and the peeled, headless, raw shrimp. Simmer for 5 minutes, or until the fish fillet pieces and the shrimp are just cooked enough, but not too much. Finish with the freshly squeezed lemon juice and serve. Serves 4.

Note: If you buy your fish cleaned and scaled, and have no Fish Stock, use chicken stock and add the shrimp heads and shells in the same way.

This is a variation of a traditional Mozambique dish called *Peixe Lumbo*.

BRAZILIAN TOMATO AND SHRIMP RICE

½ lb. shrimp, with shells and heads attached
2 cups water
2 tbsp. olive oil
1 medium onion, finely chopped
2 medium tomatoes, skinned, seeded, and finely chopped
2 large cloves garlic, minced
1 cup rice
1½ tsp. salt
¼ tsp. freshly ground black pepper
½ tsp. minced fresh habanero chili pepper, or to taste

Peel, head, and devein the shrimp and put the shrimp, shells, and heads in a saucepan with the water. Bring to a low boil and cook 10 minutes. Strain the shrimp and reserve the cooking water. Discard the heads and shells. Rough-chop the shrimp.

In the same saucepan, heat the olive oil and sauté the onions until they begin to color. Add the tomatoes, garlic, rice, and reserved shrimp water. Season with the salt, freshly ground black pepper, and habanero pepper.

Bring to a boil, cover, and turn down to a simmer and cook for 20 minutes, or until almost all the liquid has been absorbed by the rice. Spoon the chopped shrimp over the rice, cover, and cook for 10 more minutes. Fluff up the rice, turning in the now cooked shrimp, and adjust seasonings, if desired. Cook for a minute or more, uncovered, to dry out the rice if it is still too wet. Serves 4.

Note: More habanero pepper, or other available fresh hot pepper, can be used in this recipe. The heat is to your own palate.

A nice finish would be a sprinkle of a teaspoon or two of chopped parsley, chopped cilantro, or chopped green onions, or a combination of all three.

BALSAMIC VINEGAR STEAMED SALMON FILLETS WITH TOMATOES AND ONIONS

2 large onions, skinned
4 medium tomatoes, stemmed
2 tbsp. butter
Salt to taste
Black pepper, freshly ground, to taste
6 large garlic cloves, chopped
4 6-8-oz. salmon fillets
½ cup white wine
¼ cup balsamic vinegar
3 cups hot, fluffy, cooked white rice
1½ tbsp. chopped parsley
1 lemon or lime, quartered

Slice the onions crosswise into ½" thick rounds.

Slice the tomatoes crosswise into 1" thick rounds.

In a wide covered saucepan or skillet, heat the butter and lay the onion rounds into the pan to create a layer over the entire bottom of the pan. Season sparingly with salt and freshly ground black pepper. Sauté on the first side until the onions are browned on that side and turn the onions over. Sprinkle ⅓ of the garlic over the onions and season sparingly with salt and freshly ground black pepper.

Cover the onion layer with the tomato slices, sprinkle another ⅓ of the garlic over the tomatoes, and season lightly with salt and freshly ground black pepper.

Immediately lay the salmon fillets in a single layer over the tomato slices. Pour the white wine and balsamic vinegar over the fish, sprinkle them with the remaining garlic, and season sparingly with salt and freshly ground black pepper. Cover and simmer gently, basting occasionally, for about 20 minutes, or until the salmon fillets are cooked to your satisfaction.

To serve, carefully cut the cooked ingredients around each salmon fillet into the 4 portions. Slide a spatula individually under the portions and lift them from the pan onto plates held over the pan to catch the drippings. Spoon a serving of hot, fluffy white rice onto each plate and pour the pan juices over the rice and fish. Garnish the rice and fish with chopped parsley and a quarter lemon or lime. Serves 4.

Note: The liquids can be thickened at the end with ½ tsp. or so cornstarch if you want a more saucelike density.

Any flavored vinegar can be used here. Try a raspberry vinegar.

In place of the white wine you can substitute red wine, vermouth, or sherry, or ¼ cup brandy.

GRILLED REDFISH
WITH CRIOLLA SALSA

4 6-8-oz. redfish fillets
Corn oil
Salt to taste
White pepper to taste
4 tsp. butter, melted
Criolla Salsa

Light the grill or barbecue pit 30 minutes before cooking. The grill must be very clean or the fish will stick to it and collect the ash. Brush the grill with oil.

Brush the rounded side of the redfish fillets with oil. This helps prevent the fish from sticking or drying out during cooking. Season both sides of the fish with salt and white pepper. Place the fillets on the grill rounded side down.

Watch the ends of the redfish fillets. When they are half white, brush oil over the top of the fish fillets and turn them over carefully. The fish will need to cook for 10 minutes per inch of thickness.

When the fish are done, remove them and place them on plates. Top each fillet with 1 tsp. melted butter.

Serve with the Criolla Salsa on the side. Serves 4.

Note: The fish can be any firm grilling fish, or smallish whole fish.

Dijon mustard—smooth or grainy—can be used in place of the Creole mustard in the Criolla Salsa.

GRILLED SHRIMP AND TOMATOES
ON SKEWERS

4 medium-sized, not overly ripe tomatoes
Salt
16 small Roma tomatoes
2 dozen large shrimp, with heads and shells still attached
16 pearl onions, or 4 small white onions, quartered
2 large green bell peppers, stemmed, seeded,
   and each sliced into eight strips or squares
½ cup butter, melted
4 lemons
Olive oil
Black pepper, freshly ground
Cayenne pepper

Slice the tomatoes crosswise into four rounds each. Salt them lightly and lay them single-layer in plates to drain their excess juices.

Take four metal or wooden skewers and load them first with one small Roma tomato, then a shrimp, a pearl onion, a slice of bell pepper, repeating the process four times for each skewer.

Juice two of the lemons and blend with the melted butter. Halve the other two lemons and set aside for garnish.

When the coals are hot and you are ready to cook, brush the loaded skewers with olive oil, salt and pepper them, and lay them on the grill. Do the same with the sliced tomatoes.

Do not let the sliced tomatoes overcook. They should be cooked without collapsing so they can act as a sound bed for the skewered ingredients to lay upon. As soon as the grilled tomato slices are cooked, about 2 minutes on each side, remove them to dinner plates, laying them four in a row, one overlapping the other, the length of the skewered ingredients.

Turn the skewers once in the cooking and cook them about 3 minutes on each side, or until all seems to be grilled to a desired doneness.

Remove the skewers from the grill and using a fork, slide the ingredients off the skewers onto the bed of grilled tomato slices on each plate. Spoon the remaining lemon-butter sauce over the grilled shrimp and vegetables and serve. Serves 4.

Note: Four cloves of pressed garlic in the lemon-butter sauce will enhance this dish considerably for garlic lovers.

Where I live in the center of the French Quarter, on the third floor of a beautiful, old, early nineteenth-century building on Rue Royale, I enjoy the use of a small balcony overlooking the courtyard in the rear of the property. It is often, especially during the summer months, that I do my cooking on an outside charcoal grill on that balcony.

In the early evenings, as the sun is setting and the light fades from bright white to a marvelous shade of blue-purple, the cooling breezes begin to flow from the Mississippi River, which is only two short blocks away, across the balcony and through my garret, cooling even the hottest of the dog days of summer.

It is on evenings like this that I most like to relax outside with friends, sip cool drinks from tall iced glasses, and grill light dinners using the products purchased that day from the old French Market, also only a few blocks away. My friends and I are all tomato fanatics. It may be something that comes with the climate; or it may be that we are fortunate to have our fabulous Creole tomatoes to eat: I am not sure. Whatever the case may be, this simple dish seems to satisfy our needs.

UGANDAN STEAMED FISH

¼ cup peanut oil
2 onions, rough-chopped
4 medium tomatoes, rough-chopped
4 cloves garlic, chopped
1 tsp. curry powder
Salt to taste
Black pepper, freshly ground, to taste
1 3-lb. fish with its head attached, scaled and eviscerated,
    or 2 1½-lb. fish
Juice of 1 lime

Heat the oil in a skillet and sauté the onions until slightly colored. Add the tomatoes, garlic, curry powder, and season with salt and freshly ground black pepper. Simmer together for 5 minutes. Lay the whole fish into the mixture in the pan, cover, and simmer gently for 20 minutes, or until the fish is cooked all the way through. Finish with the lime juice and serve. Serves 4.

TOMATO-STUFFED FLOUNDER

½ cup butter
8 green onions, chopped
1 rib celery, chopped
¼ cup flour
4 medium tomatoes, skinned, seeded, and chopped
2 tbsp. chopped parsley
¼ tsp. thyme
1 tsp. salt, or to taste
¼ tsp. powdered white pepper
⅛ tsp. cayenne pepper
2 cups crushed stale French bread
Juice from 1 lemon
2 large eggs, lightly beaten
6 1-1½ lb. flounders, drawn and scaled
Salt

Melt the butter and add the chopped green onions and celery. Sauté for 2 minutes or until they are limp. Stir in the flour and cook for 3 more minutes. Add the tomatoes, parsley, thyme, salt, white pepper, and cayenne pepper. Cook for about 5 minutes and fold in the crushed French bread. Fold and cook together until all the liquid from the tomatoes has been absorbed by the bread. Check seasonings and remove from the heat.

When the mixture has cooled slightly, add half the lemon juice and blend in the lightly beaten eggs. Rub the flounder inside and out with salt and the remaining lemon juice and stuff the tomato mixture into the flounders. Place under the broiler for 10 minutes or until the flounders are cooked completely through and the tops are browned. Serves 4.

Note: Stale or toasted sliced bread can be used in place of the French bread.

BREADED PAN-FRIED FISH FILLETS
WITH CRAYFISH CREOLE

CREOLE SAUCE

½ cup butter
1 large green bell pepper, seeded and chopped
2 large onions, chopped
2 ribs celery, finely chopped
4 large tomatoes, rough-chopped
½ cup dry white wine
6 bay leaves
½ tsp. thyme
1½ lb. crawfish tails
Salt to taste
Black pepper to taste
Cayenne pepper to taste

In a sauté pan, melt the butter and sauté the green peppers, onions, and celery for 3 minutes. Add the tomatoes, wine, bay leaves, and thyme. Simmer for 15 minutes. Add the crayfish and simmer for 5 more minutes. Season to taste with salt, black pepper, and cayenne pepper.

2 eggs
½ cup milk
4 6-oz. skinned fresh fish fillets
Salt to taste
Black pepper to taste
1 cup French bread crumbs
½ cup butter
Chopped parsley for garnish

Beat the eggs together with the milk. Lightly season the fish fillets with salt and black pepper, dip them in the egg-wash, and dredge in the bread crumbs.

Melt the butter in a skillet and sauté the fillets for 4 minutes on each side, or until they are golden brown and cooked completely through. Spoon the Creole Sauce over the fillets and sprinkle with chopped parsley. Serves 4.

FILLET OF FISH EN PAPILLOTE

4 tbsp. butter
4 tbsp. flour
½ cup chopped green onions
4 medium tomatoes, skinned, seeded, and chopped
¾ cup dry white wine
1½ cup rich Fish Stock
¼ tsp. thyme
1 tsp. salt, or to taste
¼ tsp. white pepper, or to taste
¾ lb. small raw shrimp, peeled and deveined
¾ lb. lump crabmeat
Cooking parchment, unwaxed freezer paper,
  or aluminum foil
Butter
4 6-oz. skinned fresh fish fillets

Preheat the oven to 425 degrees.

In a saucepan, melt the butter and blend in the flour. Cook together for 3 minutes. Add the green onions and tomatoes. Cook for another 5 minutes, or until the tomatoes have rendered their liquid and the green onions have become limp. Whisk in the white wine and Fish Stock and add the thyme, salt, and pepper. Bring to a boil, turn down to a simmer, and cook 10 minutes or until the sauce acquires a fairly thick consistency.

Carefully fold in the shrimp and simmer for 1 minute more, or only long enough for the shrimp to turn pink. Remove from the fire, fold in the crabmeat, and set aside to cool.

Cut 4 heart shapes from the parchment paper, ten inches long and fourteen inches wide. Lay them out flat and butter them.

When the sauce is cool and not too liquid, spoon it onto one side of each heart. Top each with a fish fillet. Fold the other side of the heart over and crimp the edges together in several small folds, beginning at the bottom point of the heart shape, all the way around the open side. Place the *papillotes* on a greased baking pan and into the oven for 20 minutes, or until the paper browns and the sauce inside is bubbling hot. Transfer to dinner plates and bring to the table. Using two forks, tear and fold open the Fillet of Fish en Papillote across the length of the top. Serves 4.

Note: When all the seafood is perfectly fresh and delicious, the marvelous perfumes that escape from the papillotes on tearing them open at the table are reward enough for having made such an effort.

This fashion of cooking *en papillote*, or "in paper," can be used for any preparation in which you want all the juices and aromas to be kept in the cooking.

POULTRY

Poultry is a major food source of the entire world. In New Orleans, in the days when the Creoles were the primary populace of the city, poultry was served every Sunday. It was the special meal of the week. On Mondays, however, the budget needed balance, so beans were served up to even things out.

In all cuisines there exists some form of poultry dish that employs tomatoes as a major ingredient. Enjoy these choice selections.

CHICKEN CREOLE

1 tsp. salt
½ tsp. ground black pepper
½ cup flour
1 2-3 lb. chicken, cut up as for frying
½ cup peanut oil
2 medium onions, rough-chopped
1 medium bell pepper, seeded and rough-chopped
3 medium tomatoes, rough-chopped
2 cloves garlic, minced
1 tbsp. minced parsley
½ tsp. paprika
½ tsp. dried thyme leaves
1 tsp. salt
½ tsp. black pepper
¼ tsp. cayenne pepper
3 cups hot cooked white rice

Blend the salt, pepper, and flour together and rub the chicken pieces with the mixture. Heat the peanut oil in a heavy, wide skillet and brown the chicken pieces on all sides. Remove the chicken with a slotted spoon and set aside.

To the same pan, add the onions and bell peppers and sauté them until the onions are transparent. Add all the remaining ingredients (except for the cooked rice). Cover and simmer together gently for 10 minutes. Add the browned chicken pieces, cover, and continue simmering gently for 20 minutes. Put the chicken on dinner plates and spoon the sauce over the chicken and the rice. Serves 4.

Note: This dish is the essential Creole recipe. The sauce, used on chicken, shrimp, crayfish, veal, etc., is the consummate Creole sauce.

In this recipe, if the tomatoes you use collapse into too much liquid in the cooking, you can thicken the sauce by adding 1-2 tbsp. cornstarch to the sauce—remove the chicken for this—and bringing the sauce to a boil for 1 minute. Return the chicken to the sauce and heat together for 3-4 minutes, or until all is good and hot.

POACHED CHICKEN AURORA

4 tbsp. butter
3 tbsp. flour
1½ cups hot Chicken Stock
1 cup tomato puree or Tomato Sauce
Salt to taste
White pepper to taste
Cayenne pepper to taste
Water
1 medium onion, sliced
1 lemon, sliced
4 bay leaves
8 whole peppercorns
4 whole allspice
2 tbsp. salt
½ tsp. cayenne pepper
3 lb. chicken

In a small saucepan, melt the butter and stir in the flour. Stir and cook until the mixture becomes foamy, about 2 minutes. Whisk in the hot Chicken Stock and bring to a boil. Add the tomato puree or Tomato Sauce and season to taste with salt, white pepper, and cayenne pepper. Simmer for 20 minutes.

In a large pan, add enough water to give you a 4" depth. Add the onion, lemon, bay leaves, peppercorns, allspice, salt, and cayenne pepper. Bring to a rolling boil for 5 minutes. Lay the chicken into the seasoned water and cook at a gentle simmer for 25 minutes, or until the flesh of the chicken is white and flaky all the way through. Carefully remove the chicken from the water, drain, quarter, and spoon the Aurora Sauce over it. Serves 4.

GRILLED CHICKEN ANDALUSIAN

¼ cup olive oil
4 cloves garlic, chopped
1 large onion, chopped
2 medium bell peppers, seeded and chopped
1 small eggplant, skinned and cut into ½" dice
¾ cup dry white wine
1 tsp. dried thyme
Salt to taste
White pepper to taste
Cayenne pepper to taste
4 tomatoes, skinned, seeded, and chopped
4 tbsp. chopped parsley, reserving 2 tbsp.
   for garnish
1 2-3 lb. chicken, cut into frying pieces
2 tbsp. melted butter

In a sauté pan, heat the olive oil and sauté the garlic until lightly browned. Add the onion and bell pepper, and sauté for 10 minutes. Add the eggplant, white wine, and thyme; season with salt, pepper, and cayenne pepper; and simmer for 15 minutes. Stir occasionally to prevent sticking and ensure even cooking. Add the tomatoes and 2 tbsp. chopped parsley, adjust seasonings, and simmer for 10 minutes.

Brush the chicken with butter and season lightly with salt and pepper. Grill for 7 minutes on each side, or to desired doneness. Spoon the Andalusian vegetable mixture onto warm plates and place some of the grilled chicken pieces in the center of each. Garnish with the remaining chopped parsley. Serves 4.

CHICKEN AND TOMATO HOPPIN' JOHN

1 cup black beans
1½ qt. water
1 tsp. Zatarain's liquid crab boil seasoning
3" piece lemon peel
3" piece orange peel
2 ¼"-thick round lemon slices
8 whole black peppercorns
6 whole allspice
1 double chicken bouillon cube
  (or two regular bouillon cubes)
1 pickled tabasco pepper, minced
1 tbsp. molasses or dark corn syrup
1 large onion, chopped
1 small bell pepper, seeded and chopped
6 cloves garlic, chopped
2 tbsp. chopped parsley
½ tsp. cumin powder
1 tsp. curry powder
1 tbsp. chili powder
½ chicken, raw or cooked
2 tbsp. Tomato Paste
3 tomatoes, stemmed and rough-chopped
1 cup raw brown rice
1 tsp. salt

In a saucepan, add the water to the black beans and sit on the heat to simmer. Add the Zatarain's crab boil, the lemon and orange peel, the two lemon slices, the peppercorns, the allspice, the chicken bouillon cube, the tabasco pepper, and the molasses. Cover and simmer for 2 hours.

Add the chopped onion, bell pepper, garlic, and parsley, along with the cumin, curry, and chili powder. Add the chicken and simmer for 15 minutes or until the meat of the chicken is tender and can be easily removed from the carcass.

Transfer the chicken to a plate and strip the meat from the bones. Discard the bones and return the chicken to the beans. Add the Tomato Paste, chopped tomatoes, and the rice. Add the salt and bring all back to a gentle simmer. Cover and cook for 40 minutes, or until all the liquid is absorbed and the brown ice is completely cooked. You may find that the rice is cooked and there are still too many liquids left in the saucepan, in which case remove the cover and simmer until a dry enough mixture is reached. Serves 4.

Note: This is a dish that can be found both in the Southern United States as well as in the Caribbean islands. This version includes the chicken, which makes it more substantial than most.

CHICKEN AND TOMATO MAQUE CHOUX

2 tbsp. bacon drippings or melted butter
2 onions, chopped
1 bell pepper, seeded and chopped
3 cups diced roast chicken meat
4 cups fresh corn kernels
4 tomatoes, skinned, seeded, and chopped
¼ tsp. marjoram
Salt to taste
Black pepper, freshly ground, to taste

In a saucepan, heat the bacon drippings or butter and sauté the chopped onions and bell pepper until they begin to brown. Add the chicken, corn, and tomatoes. Season with marjoram, salt, and pepper; cover the pan; and simmer for 15 minutes. Serves 4.

Note: Maque choux is French for "mock cabbage." In the early days of the building of New Orleans, cabbage was scarce in the Creole vegetable gardens, so dishes that called for cabbage were often made with the more plentiful corn.

CHICKEN BREAST
WITH CREOLE SAUCE EN PAPILLOTE

3 cups Creole Sauce
4 skinless chicken breast halves
Salt to taste
Black pepper, freshly ground, to taste
Cayenne pepper to taste
Cooking parchment, unwaxed freezer paper,
  or aluminum foil
Butter

Preheat the oven to 425 degrees.

Prepare the Creole Sauce and hold aside to cool.

Rub the skinless chicken breast halves with salt, freshly ground black pepper, and cayenne pepper to taste. Hold aside.

Cut 4 heart shapes from the parchment paper, ten inches long and fourteen inches wide. Lay them out flat and rub them with butter. Spoon the Creole Sauce onto the center of one side of the parchment hearts. Top each with a seasoned skinless chicken breast half. Fold the other side of the heart over and crimp the edges together in several small folds all the way around the open side.

Place the *papillotes* on a greased baking pan and into the oven for 20 minutes, or until the paper browns and the sauce inside is bubbly hot. Remove to dinner plates and bring to the table. Using two forks, tear and fold open the Chicken Breasts with Creole Sauce en Papillote across the length of the top. Serves 4.

Note: The phrase *en papillote* is French for "in paper." The marvelous perfumes that escape from the *papillotes* on tearing them open at the table are reward enough for having made such an effort.

CHICKEN MARENGO

2 tsp. salt
1 tsp. freshly ground black pepper
¾ cup flour
¼ cup olive oil
3 tbsp. butter
1 2½-lb. chicken, cut up into 8 pieces, as for frying
1 cup chicken stock
2 dozen pearl onions or
  1 dozen small white onions, peeled
1 small green bell pepper, stemmed, seeded,
  and cut into thin strips
6 medium-sized ripe tomatoes, peeled, seeded,
  and quartered
¾ cup black olives, pitted
⅛ tsp. ground allspice
4 oz. fresh mushrooms, sliced
½ cup white wine
1 oz. (2 tbsp.) Cognac or brandy

Rub the chicken pieces with the salt and pepper and dredge them in the flour.

In a covered skillet, heat the olive oil and 2 tbsp. of the butter. Add the chicken pieces and sauté them until nicely browned. Add the chicken stock, onions, bell pepper strips, tomatoes, black olives, and ground allspice. Cover the pan and gently simmer its contents for about 45 minutes, or until the chicken is very tender.

In a small sauté pan, heat the remaining butter and sauté the sliced mushrooms briefly. Deglaze the pan with the white wine and add the mushrooms and the liquids to the chicken pan. Add the Cognac or brandy. Cover and simmer for 5 more minutes. Serves 4.

Note: It is said that Napoleon, at the battle of Marengo, on June 14, 1800, did as he was accustomed to, and waited until the battle was decided before he would have his cook prepare his meal. After Napoleon had defeated the Austrians there, his chef, Dunand, had few provisions from which to draw. The supply wagons had not caught up to the troops and thus the chef had very little with which to prepare the meal. A pilfered chicken from a nearby farm became the main ingredient of the meal, as well as a few tomatoes found growing nearby, with mushrooms from the ground and the remaining ingredients scavenged from others in the camp. Of course, Napoleon never traveled without his Cognac, so that ingredient was readily available.

This recipe has been developed to improve on that improvised battlefield presentation.

THE TOMATO COOKBOOK

MEATS

In this meat section, I have attempted to illustrate the varied international concepts of tomato-meat dishes that are some of the most popular in the countries from which they come.

They are all specialties of their respective birthplaces and the first offerings that a traveler would meet in the enjoyment of dining.

DAUBE OF BEEF

2 tbsp. oil
1½ lb. beef flank steak
2 medium onions
1 rib celery, chopped
6 cloves garlic, chopped
2 cups red wine
4 large tomatoes, skinned, seeded,
   and rough-chopped
2 tbsp. Tomato Paste
¼ cup chopped parsley
1 tsp. dried thyme
4 bay leaves
Salt to taste
Black pepper, freshly ground, to taste
1 tbsp. vinegar
Rice or pasta

Heat the oil in a skillet and sauté the beef flank steak until it is nicely browned. Add the chopped onions, celery, and garlic and continue cooking until they begin to color. Add the red wine, tomatoes, Tomato Paste, parsley, thyme, and bay leaves. Season to taste with salt and freshly ground black pepper and add the vinegar. Cover the skillet and simmer gently for one hour, or until the sauce is reduced and the steak is very tender. Cut or tear the steak into pieces and serve with rice or pasta, and the gravy poured over the dish. Serves 4.

Note: Daube is a familiar dish in Creole cuisine, although it originates in French cuisine and is in Spanish cuisine.

The word *daube* comes from the Spanish *dobar*, meaning "to braise," while *daube* in French describes a beef joint or steak braised in red wine. It is a southern French specialty and was brought here early in Louisiana's history, as were many southern specialties from France.

PICADILLO-STUFFED TOMATO IN SALSA ROJA

2 cups Salsa Roja (Roasted Anaheim Chili
    and Tomato Sauce)
⅛ tsp. ground cinnamon
⅛ tsp. ground cloves
3 cups Oaxacan Picadillo (see recipe below)
Oil for frying
8 large green or unripe tomatoes,
    interiors scooped out
⅓ cup flour
4 eggs
½ tsp. salt
1 tbsp. flour
1 tbsp. chopped cilantro for garnish

Prepare the Salsa Roja and add the cinnamon and cloves. Hold aside warm. Prepare the Oaxacan Picadillo. Hold aside. In an iron skillet or frying pan, heat enough oil to reach a ½" depth in the bottom of the pan to 375 degrees. Spoon the picadillo into the tomatoes until they are full, yet can still be closed. Seal them closed with toothpicks. Dredge the stuffed tomatoes in the flour.

Separate the eggs, add the salt to the whites, and beat them to the soft-peak stage. Beat the yolks separately and fold them into the whites along with 1 tbsp. flour. Dip the tomatoes into the egg-batter and be sure to completely coat them on all sides. Lay the battered tomatoes into the oil and fry until browned on the one side, turn over, and fry until browned on the other. Drain on absorbent paper and hold warm in the oven until all are cooked. Place two tomatoes on each plate and sauce with the Salsa Roja. Garnish with chopped cilantro. Serves 4.

OAXACAN PICADILLO

4 medium Roasted Tomatoes
1½ tbsp. bacon drippings, lard, or oil
1 large onion, skinned and chopped
2 large cloves garlic, minced
1½ lb. pork, rough-ground
⅓ cup raisins
1½ tbsp. vinegar
1 tsp. ground cinnamon
⅛ tsp. ground cloves
Salt to taste
Black pepper, freshly ground, to taste
½ cup sliced almonds, roasted
Cilantro for garnish

Stem, skin, and chop the Roasted Tomatoes and process them into a puree in a blender or food mill. Hold aside.

In a large iron skillet or sauté pan, heat the bacon drippings, lard, or oil and sauté onions and garlic until they just begin to color. Add the ground pork and cook, stirring frequently, until cooked completely through and lightly browned.

Add the tomato puree, raisins, vinegar, cinnamon, and cloves and season to taste with salt and freshly ground black pepper. Simmer for 30 minutes, or until the liquids are reduced and the ingredients have become a mass thick enough to hold its own shape. Add the roasted almonds and adjust seasonings if desired. Makes about 3½ cups.

Note: Add a little water if necessary to liquify the tomato puree.

Oaxacan Picadillo: The word *Picadillo* derives from the Spanish *picar*, or "to mince."

OSSO BUCCO MILANESE

4 large tomatoes
1 large onion
4 large cloves garlic
1 rib celery
2½ lb. veal shank (knuckle),
    cut crosswise into 8 pieces
Salt to taste
Black pepper, freshly ground, to taste
¾ cup flour
¼ cup olive oil
1 cup dry white wine
2 tbsp. chopped parsley
4 bay leaves
1 tsp. dried (1 tbsp. fresh) oregano
1 tsp. dried (1 tbsp. fresh) rosemary
1 tsp. dried (1 tbsp. fresh) sweet basil
Buttered rice or pasta
Chopped parsley for garnish

Skin and seed the tomatoes and chop them coarsely, reserving all juices and jelly. Finely chop the onion, chop the garlic, and mince the celery. Hold aside. Season the veal shank cuts liberally with salt and freshly ground black pepper and dredge in the flour.

In a wide skillet, heat the olive oil and sauté the veal shank pieces until nicely browned on both sides. Add the onions, garlic, and celery and cook until they brown lightly. Add the white wine, parsley, bay leaves, oregano, rosemary, and basil. Simmer very gently for one hour or until the sauce is well reduced and the meat of the osso bucco is fork-tender.

Serve the Osso Bucco Milanese with buttered rice or pasta garnished with chopped parsley. The marrow is the prize morsel of the shank and should be scooped out with small spoons or forks. Serves 4.

STIR-FRIED BEAN CURD
WITH TOMATO AND BEEF

1 lb. flank steak
2 tbsp. soy sauce
2 tbsp. oyster sauce
2 tbsp. sugar
2 tbsp. cornstarch
2 tbsp. sesame oil
Dash ($1/16$ tsp.) white pepper
$1/2$ cup peanut oil
1 lb. firm bean curd
4 cloves garlic, sliced crosswise, paper-thin
2 tbsp. dry sherry
4 green onions, julienned
4 medium tomatoes, skinned and seeded
$1\frac{1}{2}$ tsp. salt
$1\frac{1}{2}$ tbsp. sugar
$1\frac{1}{2}$ tbsp. cornstarch mixed with 2 tbsp.
   cold water

Cut the meat into 1" cubes and slice very thin. In a bowl, combine the meat with the soy sauce, oyster sauce, 2 tbsp. sugar, 2 tbsp. cornstarch, 1 tbsp. sesame oil, the white pepper, and 2 tbsp. of the peanut oil.

Drain the bean curd and cut into 1" cubes and then into $1/4$" slices.

Heat a wok or deep sauté pan very hot and add the remaining peanut oil. Add the garlic and beef and stir-fry for about 2 minutes. Carefully add the sherry and green onions, then using slotted spoon, remove the beef to a plate. Now add the tomatoes and stir fry 2 minutes. Add the bean curd slices, salt, and sugar. Add the cornstarch mixed with the water, stir it into the ingredients, and continue to stir and cook until the liquids thicken. Stir in the remaining sesame oil and cooked meat and heat until hot. Serves 4.

GHANA STEWED TOMATOES
AND SPINACH WITH PORK

¼ cup peanut oil
1 onion, chopped
½ lb. ground pork or beef
1 cup water or chicken stock
4 tomatoes, diced
¼ cup Tomato Paste
1 lb. fresh spinach, washed and chopped
½ tsp. dry mustard
½ tsp. ground coriander
¼ tsp. cayenne pepper, or to taste
Salt to taste
3 cups hot cooked white rice

In a skillet, heat the peanut oil and sauté the onions and meat until they begin to color. Add the water or stock, tomatoes, Tomato Paste, spinach, mustard, coriander, and cayenne pepper. Salt to taste. Cover the skillet and simmer gently for 30 minutes. Serve over rice. Serves 4.

SAUCES,
DRESSINGS,
AND STOCKS

There is hardly an area of cookery that the tomato lends itself more excellently than in the area of sauces, dressings, and stocks. The color and texture of the tomato, as well as its taste, have given it the properties to be compatible with almost any food, in any variety of sauce preparations.

AFRICAN GROUNDNUT SAUCE

¼ cup peanut oil
1 small onion, chopped
3 medium tomatoes, diced
1 small eggplant, skinned and diced
¾ cup roasted shelled peanuts
¼ cup water
2 tsp. sugar
Salt

In a skillet or sauté pan, heat the peanut oil and sauté the chopped onion until it becomes limp. Add the tomatoes and eggplant and simmer for 10 minutes. Process the peanuts in a blender into a paste with the water and sugar. Add to the pan. Simmer gently for 30 minutes. Season to taste with salt. Serve over brown or white rice, grits, white or sweet potatoes, plantains, or stewed tomatoes. Makes 3 cups.

SAUCE ANDALOUSE

1 cup Mayonnaise
4 tbsp. tomato puree
1 small red bell pepper, cut into thin julienne strips

In a small mixing bowl, combine the Mayonnaise with the tomato puree and the julienned red bell pepper. Cover and refrigerate.

This sauce is an accompaniment for cold poached or steamed fish, cold chicken, cold pork or veal, or eggs. Makes 1¾ cups.

Note: The bell pepper can be roasted or cooked before being added to the Mayonnaise if you want a milder flavor from the pepper.

ANTIBES SAUCE

1 cup Mayonnaise
2 tbsp. Tomato Paste
2 tsp. anchovy paste, or finely minced anchovy
½ tsp. dried tarragon, or 1½ tsp. chopped fresh
or vinegar-packed tarragon leaves

In a small bowl, combine thoroughly the Mayonnaise with the Tomato Paste, anchovy paste or finely minced anchovy, and tarragon. Cover tightly or transfer to a jar and refrigerate for an hour or so before using to allow the flavors to meld together.

If you are using dried tarragon, it would be best to allow the sauce to chill overnight to give the herb more time to expand its flavor. Makes 1 cup.

Note: The amount of Tomato Paste, tarragon, and anchovy can be varied to suit your own taste. I happen to be particularly fond of anchovies and prefer more than prescribed in the recipe. You decide what you like the best.

Antibes Sauce is served with steamed or boiled seafood, chicken, or vegetables—cooked and raw. Or, try it on sliced hard-boiled eggs with perhaps a garnish of a few capers and paprika.

The village of Antibes is located on the French Riviera near the larger city of Nice. It is, for the most part, an exclusive residential/resort area where the wealthy French keep many elegant summer homes for their private use.

The restaurants and hotel dining rooms there are ready to serve up dishes with this sauce, there called Sauce Antiboise, at any moment, particularly in the latter part of the summer when the weather is its hottest and the villas are jammed-packed with families and friends making the most of their holiday.

AURORA SAUCE

3 tbsp. butter
2 tbsp. flour
1 cup hot Fish Stock
¾ cup tomato puree or Tomato Sauce
1 tbsp. butter
Salt to taste
White pepper to taste
Cayenne pepper to taste

In a small saucepan, melt the butter and stir in the flour. Stir and cook until the mixture becomes foamy, about 2 minutes. Whisk in the hot stock and bring to a boil. Add the tomato puree or Tomato Sauce and season to taste with salt, white pepper, and cayenne pepper. Simmer for 20 minutes. Serve with poached fish, chicken, eggs, or vegetables. Makes 1¾ cups.

BEEF STOCK

10 lb. beef and veal bones and scraps
4 onions, sliced
3 carrots, sliced
2 stalks celery
1 bell pepper, seeded and quartered
4 bay leaves
½ bunch parsley
1 gallon water

Brown the bones and scraps, onions, and carrots in the bottom of a stock pot, and add all remaining ingredients. Simmer for 4 hours, skimming the fat off the top from time to time. Strain and reduce to two quarts. Use as a base in sauces and soups. Makes 2 quarts.

BON TON SAUCE

½ cup Mayonnaise
½ cup ketchup
½ tsp. minced garlic
1 tsp. prepared horseradish
2 tbsp. white vinegar

In a bowl, combine the Mayonnaise with the ketchup, garlic, horseradish, and white vinegar. Transfer to a jar, cap tightly, and refrigerate until ready to use. Serve with fried tomatoes or seafood, or as a dressing for salad. Makes 1 good cup.

BOILED BEEF SAUCE TUJAGUE

½ cup ketchup
¼ cup Creole mustard
¼ cup prepared horseradish

In a bowl, combine the ketchup, Creole mustard, and horseradish until they are well blended. Serve at room temperature. Store the sauce in a tightly capped jar in the refrigerator to keep the horseradish from losing its flavor. Serve with boiled beef, or with cold leftover meats and poultry. Makes 1 cup.

COCKTAIL SAUCE

¾ cup ketchup
¼ cup prepared horseradish
¼ cup fresh lemon juice
1 tsp. Louisiana hot sauce, or to taste

Combine all ingredients and store tightly capped in a jar in the refrigerator. Cocktail Sauce is used with cold boiled seafood or raw oysters. Makes 1¼ cups.

COLBERT SAUCE

½ cup Tomato Sauce
1 oz. (2 tbsp.) sherry
1½ cups warm Hollandaise Sauce

In a saucepan, combine the Tomato Sauce with the sherry and reduce slightly. Let cool slightly and blend in the warm Hollandaise. Keep warm without allowing to simmer, or the sauce will separate. Serve with eggs, poultry, fish, and seafood. Makes 2 cups.

CYPRIOTE SAUCE

½ cup Tomato Sauce
2 large hard-boiled eggs
2 anchovy fillets
1 cup Mayonnaise
¼ tsp. ground fennel seeds
Salt to taste

In a small saucepan, simmer the Tomato Sauce until it is reduced by half. Remove from the heat to cool. Shell the hard-boiled eggs and sieve them or mince them very finely. Mash the anchovies or finely mince them.

In a small bowl, blend the Mayonnaise together with the cooled reduced Tomato Sauce. Add the anchovies and ground fennel seed. Season with additional salt, if desired. Cover tightly and refrigerate for an hour, or overnight if possible, to allow the flavors to meld.

Cypriote Sauce is used with fish and seafood, eggs, and vegetables—both raw and cooked—as well as a salad dressing.

Try it on sliced, ripe, well-chilled tomatoes as a salad or a cool luncheon meal. Makes 1½ cups.

Note: The ground fennel seed is the key ingredient here that makes this sauce different from similar others. Vary its quantity, starting with less, until you find what best suits you.

The Isle of Cypress in Greece is home to this mayonnaise-based sauce.

FISH STOCK

10 lb. fish heads and bones
4 onions, sliced
4 ribs celery
6 bay leaves
½ bunch parsley
1 gallon water

In a stock pot, add all ingredients and bring to a simmer. Simmer uncovered for 4 hours and skim the surface from time to time. Strain and reduce to 2 quarts. Use as a base for soups and sauces. Makes 2 quarts.

CREOLE SAUCE

2 tbsp. butter
2 onions, rough-chopped
1 large green bell pepper, seeded and rough-chopped
4 large cloves garlic, minced
5 tomatoes, skinned, seeded, and chopped
¼ tsp. dried thyme
2 bay leaves
1 tsp. paprika
¼ tsp. cayenne pepper
Salt to taste
Black pepper, freshly ground, to taste
1 tbsp. cornstarch mixed with 2 tbsp. *cold* water
2 tbsp. minced parsley

In a saucepan, melt the butter and sauté the onions, green bell pepper, and garlic until they become limp. Add the tomatoes, thyme, bay leaves, paprika, and cayenne pepper and season to taste with salt and freshly ground black pepper. Cover and simmer gently for 20 minutes. Add the cornstarch mixed with the water and blend it into the sauce. Simmer for 2 more minutes, while stirring, until the sauce thickens. Add the minced parsley. Makes 3 cups.

Note: This sauce is the base of many of the most important dishes in New Orleans cookery. As our cuisine is Creole, this sauce is the finest example of what that description means.

Although a tomato sauce, Creole Sauce should not be overcooked into a sauce resembling an Italian tomato sauce. The vegetables should remain recognizable with the tomatoes acting as the principle ingredient.

Creole Sauce is used with almost every food one can come by. Shrimp and Chicken Creole are the most popular renditions of the dish and can be found throughout the city in many of our neighborhoods, as well as in the more elegant restaurants.

When I was growing up in New Orleans, Shrimp or Chicken Creole was a weekly staple on our family table, and a welcomed dish every time it was served. With our family of seven children, we had the luxury of having a Creole cook named Nancy Madison, who was the first to teach me the joys of Creole cuisine. It is probably due to her culinary talents that I have remained an aficionado of Creole cookery and continue to research the subject and document my findings in the eight cookbooks that I have written to date.

DEMI-GLAS SAUCE

3 tbsp. butter
½ cup finely chopped onion
½ cup finely chopped carrot
3 tbsp. flour
3 cups Beef Stock
1 tbsp. Tomato Paste
2 cloves garlic, minced
½ tsp. dried thyme
1 small rib celery, minced
2 bay leaves
3 sprigs parsley
Salt to taste
Black pepper to taste

In a saucepan, melt 2 tbsp. of the butter, add the onion and carrot, and cook the vegetables until they begin to brown. Add the remaining butter, stir in the flour, and cook the roux until it is browned. Add the Beef Stock, Tomato Paste, garlic, thyme, celery, bay leaves, parsley, salt, and pepper. Bring the mixture to a boil and simmer for 30 minutes. Strain and hold aside. Serve with meats or use as a sauce base. Makes 3 cups.

MADEIRA SAUCE

¾ cup butter
6 tbsp. flour
2 cups beef stock or bouillon
½ cup Madeira wine
Salt to taste
Black pepper to taste

In a saucepan, melt the butter and blend in the flour. Cook over low heat, stirring constantly, until the roux turns a medium brown, approximately 12 to 15 minutes. Whisk in the stock or bouillon and add the Madeira wine. Season to taste with salt and black pepper and simmer for 5 minutes or so. Makes 3½ cups.

POYDRAS SAUCE

¾ cup tomato catsup
¼ cup Dijon mustard
2 tbsp. grated onion
1½ tbsp. Worcestershire sauce
½ tsp. paprika
Salt to taste
Louisiana hot sauce to taste

Blend all ingredients together, seasoning to taste with salt and hot sauce. Store, covered, in the refrigerator. Makes 1¼ cups.

Poydras Sauce goes best with cold meats and poultry, but is also used with cold seafood.

RUSSIAN TOMATO DRESSING

½ cup **Tomato Mayonnaise**
½ cup **Tomato Catsup**
2 tbsp. **minced celery**
2 tbsp. **minced green onions**
1 tbsp. **minced parsley**
¼ cup **red lumpfish roe**
¼ tsp. **white pepper**

In a small bowl, fold the Tomato Mayonnaise together with the Tomato Catsup. Add the celery, green onions, and parsley and blend all together well. Add the red lumpfish roe and continue to fold all together carefully without crushing the roe eggs. Season with white pepper to taste. Makes 1½ cups.

Note: Salt is already in the Tomato Mayonnaise and the Tomato Catsup, and the lumpfish roe is heavily salted. There should be no need for additional salt in this dressing. Try this with the Tomato, Avocado, and Red Onion Salad.

ROASTED ANAHEIM CHILI AND TOMATO SAUCE

4 large **Anaheim chilies, seeded and chopped**
3 cloves **garlic, mashed**
2 large **Roasted Tomatoes**
Water, if necessary
Salt to taste

Cut the chilies into flat pieces and cook in a heated skillet for about 30 seconds on each side with the garlic. Peel and seed the Roasted Tomatoes. Place the cooked ingredients in a blender and process into a smooth puree. Add a little water if necessary to process the ingredients. Season with salt and let it sit for 30 minutes before serving. Makes 1½ cups.

Note: This is a *salsa roja*. It is used with meats and poultry. It is most often served room temperature as a condiment.

MAYONNAISE

1 whole large egg
½ tsp. salt
¼ tsp. ground white pepper
⅛ tsp. cayenne pepper
1 cup peanut, olive, or corn oil
2 tbsp. lemon juice

In a bowl, begin the Mayonnaise by beating the egg, salt, white pepper, and cayenne pepper together with 1 tbsp. of the oil. Continue whisking in the oil, 1 tbsp. at a time, until the sauce has emulsified and all oil is incorporated into the sauce. Now add the lemon juice and adjust seasonings to your taste. Store the Mayonnaise tightly covered in the refrigerator. Makes approximately 1½ cups.

Note: An important singular sauce, Mayonnaise is used in many different ways—as a base for many other sauces and as an ingredient in numerous recipe preparations.

TOMATO MAYONNAISE

1 medium ripe tomato, skinned and seeded
1 whole large egg
½ tsp. salt
¼ tsp. ground white pepper
⅛ tsp. cayenne pepper
1 cup peanut, olive, or corn oil
1 tbsp. Tomato Paste
2 tbsp. lemon juice

Puree the tomato pulp and hold aside. In a bowl, begin the Mayonnaise by beating the egg, salt, ground white pepper, and cayenne pepper together with 1 tbsp. of the oil. Continue whisking in the oil, a tablespoon at a time, until the sauce has emulsified and all the oil is incorporated into the sauce.

Fold in the pureed tomato and Tomato Paste. Add the lemon juce and adjust seasonings to your taste. Store the Tomato Mayonnaise tightly covered in the refrigerator. Makes approximately 2 cups.

Note: An important singular sauce, Tomato Mayonnaise is used in many different ways—as a base for many other sauces and as an ingredient in many recipe preparations.

SPANISH SAUCE

3 tbsp. butter
½ cup finely chopped onion
½ cup finely chopped carrot
3 tbsp. flour
3 cups beef or chicken stock
1 cup Tomato Sauce
2 cloves garlic, minced
½ tsp. thyme
1 small stalk celery
2 bay leaves
3 sprigs parsley
1 tsp. sugar
1 tsp. water
3 tbsp. vinegar
¼ tsp. anchovy paste
Salt to taste
Black pepper to taste

In a saucepan, melt the butter and sauté the onion and carrot until they begin to color. Add the flour and cook until brown. Add the stock, Tomato Sauce, garlic, thyme, celery, bay leaves, and parsley.

In another small saucepan, caramelize the sugar with the water; remove from heat and immediately add the vinegar. Mix in the anchovy paste, add this mixture to the ingredients of the other saucepan, and bring to a simmer. Season to taste with salt and pepper, cover, and simmer for 30 minutes. Pass the sauce through a strainer and hold warm. Makes 2 cups.

Note: This sauce is known as Espagnole in traditional French cuisine. It is used as a sauce for meats, pasta, rice, vegetables, and poultry, as well as a base for other sauces.

TOMATETTE DRESSING

2 tbsp. red wine vinegar
2 tbsp. lemon juice
1 tsp. salt, or to taste
2 tbsp. Dijon or Creole mustard
½ tsp. white pepper, or to taste
⅔ cup olive oil
½ cup fresh tomato puree
2 tbsp. Tomato Paste

In a small mixing bowl, combine the red wine vinegar, lemon juice, and salt and stir until the salt dissolves. Add the Dijon or Creole mustard and white pepper and whisk in the olive oil in a steady stream. Blend in the tomato puree and Tomato Paste. Adjust seasonings to suit your taste. Bottle, cap tightly, and refrigerate until used. Makes 1½ cups.

TOMATO BUTTER

1 medium ripe tomato, rough-chopped
1 tbsp. minced French shallot,
    or the white part of green onion
½ cup butter

In a small sauté pan, heat 2 tbsp. of the butter and sauté the tomato and French shallot or green onion. Cook until the tomato has released its juices and the liquid has mostly evaporated. Remove from the heat and pass the mixture through a strainer.

In the same saucepan, melt the remaining butter without allowing it to come to a simmer. Add the cooked tomato mixture and heat together gently without letting the sauce come to a simmer.

Serve with eggs, fish, and poultry, as well as grilled or fried tomatoes. Tomato Butter also makes a nice sauce for baked, stuffed tomato dishes. Makes ¾ cup.

Note: You can substitute 1-2 tbsp. Tomato Paste here for the fresh tomato.

TOMATO AND CHILI SAUCE

4 medium Roasted Tomatoes, peeled and seeded
4 Serranos chilies, stemmed and seeded
1 medium onion, skinned and chopped
3 cloves garlic, peeled and chopped
2 tbsp. bacon drippings or oil
Salt to taste

Put the tomatoes, chilies, onion, and garlic in a blender or food processor and process to a rough puree. Heat the bacon drippings or oil in a skillet until fairly hot and add the vegetable puree. Cook while stirring constantly for about 10-12 minutes, or until the sauce colors and thickens. Season with salt to taste. Makes 2 cups.

Note: Serve with egg, rice, pork, or Mexican dishes.

TOMATO SAUCE

¼ cup olive oil
1 onion, chopped
3 cloves garlic, chopped
½ rib celery, chopped
8 medium tomatoes, chopped
2 tbsp. minced fresh sweet basil leaves
2 tbsp. minced parsley leaves
Salt to taste
Black pepper, freshly ground, to taste

In a saucepan, heat the olive oil and add the onions, garlic, and celery. Sauté until they become translucent. Add the tomatoes, basil, parsley, salt, and pepper. Cook only long enough for the tomatoes to collapse into a thick yet liquid state. Strain the sauce through a sieve. Makes 1 quart.

Note: Use as a sauce on seafood, pasta, eggs, poultry, meats, or almost anything that you cook. Use as the base for soups and other sauces.

TOMATO CLAM SAUCE

2 tbsp. olive oil
1 large onion, finely chopped
1 tbsp. flour
3 medium tomatoes, skinned, seeded,
**   and finely chopped**
4 large cloves minced garlic
1 tbsp. minced fresh basil leaves
½ tsp. dried oregano leaves
1 cup chopped clams, fresh or canned
Salt to taste
Black pepper, freshly ground, to taste
2 tbsp. chopped parsley

In a skillet, heat the olive oil and add the onions. Sauté them until they are lightly browned and blend in the flour. Stir and cook for 1 minute, then add the tomatoes, garlic, basil, and oregano. Cover and simmer for 15 minutes, or until the tomatoes are cooked into the sauce.

Just before serving, add the clams and season with salt and freshly ground black pepper. Cook only long enough for the clam pieces to be cooked but not yet tough. Blend in the parsley and serve over pasta. Makes approximately 2½ cups.

Note: If you use fresh clams, cook them for only a moment, or for very long. They become tough and rubbery anywhere in between.

The clams can be substituted with fresh chopped oysters, which are far easier to come by in the South than fresh clams.

This sauce can be served with any choice of pasta, fresh or dried. Or try it over Tomato Rice for a kind of Italian paella entree.

TOMATO PASTE

2 qt. (8 cups) skinned and chopped very ripe tomatoes,
**   all released liquids and jelly reserved**

In a saucepan, heat the tomatoes, bringing them to a simmer, and simmer them until they are reduced by half, approximately 30 minutes.

Carefully strain the reduced tomatoes through a fine sieve or cheesecloth and return to the heat. Reduce a little more, simmering very gently, until the tomatoes thicken into a paste consistency. Transfer into a covered jar and store in the refrigerator. Makes 1 cup.

Note: The Tomato Paste will keep for weeks in the refrigerator if properly capped in a jar.

TOMATO RED WINE SAUCE

3 tbsp. butter
3 tbsp. flour
1 onion, minced
½ cup minced fresh mushrooms
1 medium carrot, minced
1 medium stalk celery, minced
1 whole head garlic, peeled and minced
2 cups fresh tomato puree
2 tbsp. minced parsley
2 bay leaves
½ tsp. thyme
1 cup dry red wine
1 cup rich beef broth or stock
1 tsp. salt
½ tsp. black pepper

In a saucepan, melt the butter and blend in the flour. Cook together until it begins to brown, then add the minced onion, mushrooms, carrot, celery, and garlic. Cook together until browned, then add the remaining ingredients. Simmer gently for 45 minutes. Makes 2 cups.

Note: This sauce is best served with beef and other meat dishes.

VELOUTE SAUCE WITH FISH FUME AND WHITE WINE

¾ lb. fish heads and bones
1 cup chopped onions
½ cup sliced mushrooms
1 tbsp. lemon juice
1 tsp. salt
8 black peppercorns
2 sprigs parsley
¼ tsp. thyme
2 cups water
1 cup white wine
3 tbsp. butter
3 tbsp. flour

In a saucepan, place the fish heads and bones, onions, mushrooms, lemon juice, salt, peppercorns, parsley, thyme, water, and wine in a soup pot, and simmer for 30 minutes. Strain through a fine sieve.

In a heavy saucepan, melt the butter, blend in the flour, and cook over medium heat for 3 minutes or until the flour is cooked. Whisk in the strained stock and simmer for 10 minutes or until the sauce has thickened. Hold warm. Makes 2 cups.

SALSAS AND CONDIMENTS

The tomato provides an unequaled foundation for the building of sauces and condiments. Its pulpy consistency supplies texture, its color provides visual attractiveness, and its flavor provides the true pleasure of its use.

Tomatoes are used worldwide as the base for countless salsa and condiment recipes.

CRIOLLA SALSA

2 medium tomatoes, seeded and chopped
1 small onion, chopped
½ small cucumber, peeled, seeded, and chopped
¼ medium green bell pepper, seeded and chopped
1 clove garlic, minced
2 tsp. capers, minced
2 tbsp. minced parsley
½ tsp. minced fresh tarragon leaves
2 tbsp. Creole mustard
1½ tbsp. red wine vinegar
1 tbsp. olive oil
¼ tsp. salt, or to taste
¼ tsp. cayenne pepper, or to taste

In a bowl, combine the tomatoes, onion, cucumber, green bell pepper, garlic, capers, parsley, tarragon leaves, Creole mustard, red wine vinegar, and olive oil. Season to taste with salt and cayenne pepper. Cover and chill in the refrigerator, but do not store overnight or the vegetables will lose their crispness and the salsa will become flat in texture. Makes approximately 1¾ cups.

MEXICAN SALSA

2 medium ripe tomatoes
2 jalapeño peppers
1 medium yellow onion
2 cloves garlic, minced
¼ cup chopped fresh cilantro leaves
1 tsp. cider vinegar
Salt to taste

Finely chop or mince all vegetables and combine in a bowl. Add the vinegar and salt to taste. Allow to stand for 30 minutes to allow flavors to meld. Makes 1¾ cups.

Note: Serrano chilies can be used in place of the jalapeños. Lime juice can be used in place of the vinegar.

TOMATO SALSA

1 cup chopped ripe tomatoes
½ cup chopped onions
¼ cup freshly squeezed lime juice
2 tbsp. minced cilantro
1½ tbsp. minced mild green chili pepper
1 tsp. minced jalapeño pepper
1 small clove garlic, minced
½ tsp. salt

In the vessel of a food processor or blender, combine the tomatoes, onions, lime juice, cilantro, green chili pepper, jalapeño pepper, garlic, and salt. Process to a rough puree. Check for saltiness and heat and adjust to suit your own palate. Cover and chill in the refrigerator for several hours or overnight, if possible. Makes 2 cups.

Serve with Mexican and Southwestern cuisine or with grilled meats and fish. It also serves well as a condiment to bean and couscous dishes.

Note: Tomato Paste and/or tomato juice can be used to adjust taste and consistency of the salsa.

TOMATO AND RED ONION SALSA

2 medium tomatoes, seeded and finely chopped
1 medium red onion, skinned and finely chopped
¼ cup red wine vinegar
1 tsp. Louisiana hot sauce
¼ tsp. salt, or to taste

In a small bowl, combine the tomato with the red onion. Add the red wine vinegar and Louisiana hot sauce and salt to taste. Serve at room temperature with bean dishes or fish dishes. Makes 1½ cups.

YUCATECAN TOMATO AND HABANERO SALSA

2 medium ripe tomatoes
1 or 2 habanero peppers
1 medium red onion
¼ cup chopped fresh cilantro leaves
3 tsp. lime or bitter orange juice
Salt to taste

Chop all vegetables and combine in a bowl. Add the lime or bitter orange juice and season to taste with salt. Allow to stand for 30 minutes or more before serving. Makes 1¾ cups.

Note: This salsa recipe comes from the Yucatan Peninsula of Mexico, where it is called *Xnipic*, which translates as "dog's nose."

TOMATO CATSUP

1 gallon chopped ripe tomatoes
1 qt. chopped onions
1½ cups brown sugar
1 cup cider vinegar
¼ cup salt
1½ tsp. ground cinnamon
1½ tsp. ground allspice
1½ tsp. ground cloves
½ tsp. ground cayenne
2 tsp. ground dry mustard

In a pot, combine the tomatoes and onions, cover, and cook until soft, about 15 minutes. Force the mixture through a strainer or puree in a food processor or blender. Return to the pan and add remaining ingredients. Bring to a simmer and cook for an hour and a half, or until the catsup has reached a thick enough consistency. Transfer to hot sterilized bottles or jars and seal. Makes 4-5 pints.

GREEN TOMATO-MANGO CHUTNEY

4 cups diced green tomatoes
2 cups peeled diced green mango
3 sweet green bell peppers, seeded and chopped
2 medium onions, chopped
2 cups brown sugar
2 cups vinegar
½ tsp. allspice
½ tsp. clove
½ tsp. cinnamon
½ tsp. ginger
½ tsp. cayenne pepper
1 tsp. salt
Juice from 1 large orange
Juice from 1 large lime

In an enamel or uncoated copper saucepan, combine the green tomatoes, mango, bell peppers, and onions. Cook until all fruits and vegetables are soft. Add the brown sugar, vinegar, spices, and orange and lime juices and cook until thick. Transfer to hot sterile jars and seal. Makes 5 pints.

GREEN TOMATO CHUTNEY

4 lb. green tomatoes, diced
1 lb. onions, diced
2 tsp. minced garlic
2 tsp. mixed spice
2 cups brown sugar
1 tsp. salt
¼ tsp. cayenne pepper
1 cup vinegar

In an enamel or uncoated copper casserole or preserving pan, combine the tomatoes and onions with the garlic, mixed spice, brown sugar, salt, cayenne pepper, and vinegar. Bring to a low boil and cook until the mixture obtains a thick consistency. Adjust seasonings if desired. Transfer the chutney to hot sterilized jars and seal. Makes 5 pints.

PINEAPPLE-TOMATO CHUTNEY

1 small pineapple
2 cups tomato puree
1 cup raisins
1 onion, chopped
2 cloves garlic, minced
1½ cup vinegar
2 cups brown sugar
1 tbsp. salt
3 tbsp. minced ginger
½ cup chopped cashews

Skin and core the pineapple and cut it into small dice. Place in an enameled pot with the tomato puree, raisins, onion, garlic, and vinegar and bring to a low boil. Add the brown sugar, salt, and ginger and simmer until pineapple dice are soft. Add the chopped cashews and continue simmering until the liquid is sufficiently reduced. Transfer to sterile jars. Makes 3 pints.

CARIBBEAN TOMATO-PINEAPPLE JAM

3 cups chopped tomato meat
1 large pineapple, skinned, cored, and chunked
4 cups brown sugar
1 tsp. salt
1 tsp. allspice
Juice from 3 limes

In a food processor, process the tomato and pineapple meat to a rough pulp. Then, in an enamel or uncoated copper saucepan, combine the tomato and pineapple pulp with the brown sugar, salt, allspice, and lime juice. Simmer slowly until the mixture becomes thick as jam. Pack into sterilized pint jars and seal. Makes 6 pints.

GREEN TOMATO JAM

2 lb. green tomatoes
1¾ lb. brown sugar
1 lemon
½ tsp. salt
¼ tsp. ground cinnamon
⅛ tsp. ground cloves
½ tsp. vanilla extract

In an enamel or uncoated copper pan, combine the ingredients and cook at a low boil until the mixture acquires the consistency of jam. Allow to cool slightly and pass through a strainer. Return to the pan, bring to a boil, and then transfer to hot, sterilized, canning jars and seal. Makes 4 pints.

TOMATO-PAPAYA JAM WITH GINGER

3 cups diced tomato meat
3 cups diced, skinned papaya
½ cup lime juice
4 cups brown sugar
2 tbsp. minced fresh ginger
1 tsp. salt

In an enamel or uncoated copper saucepan, combine the tomatoes, papaya, lime juice, 2 cups of the brown sugar, the ginger, and salt. Heat while stirring until the sugar is dissolved and the juice is rendered from the fruits. Add the remaining brown sugar and simmer until thick as jam. Transfer to sterile jars. Makes 4 pints.

ITALIAN SWEET TOMATO PRESERVES

3 lb. very ripe fleshy tomatoes
¾ lb. sugar
⅓ cup water
2 lemons
1½ tsp. vanilla extract

Skin and seed the tomatoes and halve or quarter them according to their size. Put the sugar in a saucepan with the water. Heat until the sugar is melted. Add the tomatoes. Grate the zest from one lemon and add it to the pot. Squeeze the juice from both lemons and add it to the pot also. Cook, uncovered, over a low to moderate heat for about 45 minutes, reducing the mixture until it acquires the consistency of a fruit jam. Add the vanilla extract and remove from the heat to cool. Pour the preserves into a container, tightly cover, and refrigerate for several hours before using. Makes 3 pints.

Note: This is a simple little recipe for a sweet tomato preserve that can be used as you would use any preserve. Try it on buttered toast for breakfast or with a piece of cheese. After all, the tomato is a fruit and not a vegetable.

HORSERADISH PICKLED GREEN TOMATOES

2 dozen small green tomatoes
¾ cup diced fresh horseradish
2 tbsp. salt
1 qt. distilled white vinegar
1½ tbsp. whole black peppercorns
8 whole cloves
2 tbsp. mustard seed
2 tbsp. sugar

Wash and stem the tomatoes and pierce the skin in several places with the tip of a paring knife. Pack the tomatoes into sterilized canning jars, equally distributing the horseradish dice, and salting each layer as you go.

In an enamel saucepan, heat the vinegar together with the remaining ingredients without allowing the liquid to boil. Remove from heat to cool slightly. Pour the pickling liquid over the tomatoes and cap the jars with tight seals.

Allow the pickled tomatoes to stand for 10 days before using. They should keep unrefrigerated for 3-4 months. Makes 4 pints.

Note: Hot peppers can be used when fresh horseradish is not available.

FRESH GREEN TOMATO RELISH

2 large green tomatoes, finely chopped
1 tbsp. salt
½ cup finely chopped cabbage
½ cup finely chopped onion
¼ cup finely chopped sweet red bell pepper
1 cayenne, tabasco, or 2 sport peppers, minced
¼ cup minced celery
¼ cup brown sugar
½ cup vinegar
1 tbsp. mustard seeds

In a bowl, combine the tomatoes with the salt and set aside for 15 minutes to allow the salt to draw the water from the tomatoes. Add the cabbage, onion, sweet red bell pepper, cayenne or other hot pepper, celery, brown sugar, vinegar, and mustard seeds. Cover and refrigerate overnight. Serve with lamb, pork, or poultry. Makes 2¾ cups.

GREEN TOMATO AND MUSTARD PICKLE

2 cups peeled diced cucumber
2 cups diced onions
1 cup diced cauliflower
1 cup diced sweet green peppers
1 cup diced sweet red peppers
Water to cover
½ cup salt
3 cups diced green tomatoes
1 qt. vinegar
1½ cups brown sugar
½ cup flour
3 tbsp. powdered mustard
2 tsp. powdered turmeric
2 tsp. powdered ginger

In a large pan, combine the cucumbers, onions, cauliflower, green and red peppers, water, and salt. Cover and allow to stand overnight. After the overnight soaking, bring the vegetables to a boil in the pan, remove from the heat, and pour out the water. Add the tomatoes, vinegar, brown sugar, flour, mustard, turmeric, and ginger. Pour the mixture over the parboiled vegetables, bring to a boil, and cook for 10 minutes. Transfer to hot, sterilized pint jars and seal. Makes 4 pints.

TOMATO AND CORN RELISH

1 medium tomato, skinned, seeded, and chopped
Kernels from 1 ear cooked fresh corn
  (approximately ¾ cup)
1 green onion, chopped
¼ cup fresh lime juice
1 tbsp. minced fresh cilantro leaves
1 tbsp. minced fresh green chili pepper
  or mild jalapeño pepper
Salt to taste
Black pepper, freshly ground, to taste

In a bowl, combine the tomato with the corn kernels, green onion, lime juice, cilantro, and green chili pepper or jalapeño pepper. Season to taste with salt and freshly ground black pepper.

Use this relish with fish and eggs dishes, or as a condiment with bean dishes and poultry. Makes 1½ cups.

Note: This is a fresh relish that loses its crispness if kept for too long.

MUFFINS,
ROLLS, AND
DESSERTS

Tomatoes are often employed as flavorant for muffins and rolls. These recipes are simple and easily prepared. They can be enjoyed as an accompaniment to a meal, or alone.

In the few dessert recipes, the variability of the tomato shines through. The real tomato fancier will delight in these offerings.

TOMATO MUFFINS

2 cups presifted all-purpose flour
2 tbsp. sugar
1 tbsp. baking powder
¼ tsp. salt
¾ cup minced ripe tomato meat
2 tbsp. Tomato Paste
1 egg
¼ cup melted butter
1 cup milk

Preheat the oven to 400 degrees.

In a bowl, combine the flour, sugar, baking powder, and salt. Fold in the tomato meat and the Tomato Paste. In another bowl, beat the egg together with the melted butter and milk. Stir the liquid ingredients into the dry ingredients and spoon into 12 buttered muffin tins. Bake in the oven for 25 minutes or until the muffins begin to separate from the sides of the tins. Makes 1 dozen.

BACON AND TOMATO MUFFINS

2 cups presifted all-purpose flour
1½ tbsp. baking powder
1 tbsp. sugar
1 tsp. salt
1 egg
2 tbsp. melted butter
1 cup milk
¾ cup tomato puree
4 strips bacon, minced

Preheat the oven to 400 degrees.

In a bowl, combine the flour, baking powder, sugar, and salt. In another bowl, beat the egg together with the melted butter and milk. Incorporate the wet and dry mixtures until a batter has been formed.

Pour one half of the batter into 12 buttered muffin tins, spoon 1 tbsp. tomato puree onto each muffin, and top with the remaining batter. Sprinkle the minced bacon over the tops of the muffins. Bake in the oven for 25 minutes or until the muffins begin to separate from the sides of the tins. Makes 1 dozen.

TOMATO-PECAN MUFFINS

1¾ cups presifted all-purpose flour
1 tbsp. baking powder
1 tsp. salt
1 tbsp. Tomato Paste
½ cup chopped pecans
6 tbsp. butter, softened
⅔ cup sugar
2 eggs, separated
¼ cup tomato juice

Preheat the oven to 400 degrees.

In a bowl, combine the flour, baking powder, salt, Tomato Paste, and chopped pecans. In another bowl, cream the butter together with the sugar and beat in the egg yolks and tomato juice. In another bowl, beat the egg whites until stiff.

Now combine the wet ingredients with the dry ingredients and fold in the beaten egg whites. Spoon the mixture into 12 buttered muffin tins. Bake in the oven for 25 minutes. Makes 1 dozen.

TOMATO JAM CORN MUFFINS

2 cups presifted all-purpose flour
1 cup cornmeal
2 tbsp. sugar
1 tbsp. baking powder
¾ tsp. salt
1 egg
¼ cup melted butter
1 cup milk
½ cup Green Tomato Jam

Preheat the oven to 400 degrees.

In a bowl, combine the flour, cornmeal, sugar, baking powder, and salt. In another bowl, beat the egg together with the melted butter and milk. Stir the wet ingredients into the dry ingredients and spoon half of the batter into 12 buttered muffin tins. Place 1 tsp. of Green Tomato Jam on each muffin and cover with the remaining half of the batter. Bake in the oven for 25 minutes. Makes 1 dozen.

TOMATO PRESERVE CORN MUFFINS

1 cup cornmeal
1 cup presifted all-purpose flour
1 tbsp. baking powder
¾ tsp. salt
1 cup Italian Sweet Tomato Preserves
2 tbsp. butter, melted
1 egg
¾ cup milk

Preheat the oven to 400 degrees.

In a bowl, combine the cornmeal, flour, baking powder, and salt. Stir in the tomato preserves. In another bowl, beat the butter together with the egg and milk. Stir the milk and egg mixture into the flour-cornmeal-tomato preserve mixture until all is blended. Spoon the batter into 8 buttered muffin tins. Bake in the oven for 25 minutes or until the muffins begin to separate from the tins. Makes 8 muffins.

TOMATO SPICE CORN MUFFINS

1 cup presifted all-purpose flour
¾ cup cornmeal
¾ cup sugar
1 tbsp. baking powder
½ tsp. baking soda
½ tsp. salt
½ tsp. cinnamon
½ tsp. nutmeg
½ tsp. cloves
1 egg
1 cup tomato juice (see Simple Raw Tomato Juice)
2 tbsp. melted butter

Preheat the oven to 400 degrees.

In a bowl, combine the flour, cornmeal, sugar, baking powder, baking soda, salt, cinnamon, nutmeg, and cloves. In another bowl, beat the egg together with the tomato juice and melted butter. Stir the wet ingredients into the dry ingredients and pour into 12 buttered muffin tins. Bake in the oven for 25 minutes or until the muffins begin to separate from the sides of the tin. Makes 1 dozen.

TOMATO YEAST ROLLS

1 cup tomato pulp
2 tbsp. sugar
1 tsp. salt
2 tbsp. butter
2 pkg. active dry yeast
¼ cup warm water (110 degrees)
1 tsp. sugar
1 egg
3½ cups presifted all-purpose flour

In a saucepan, combine the tomato pulp, sugar, salt, and butter and bring to a simmer. Remove from heat and transfer the mixture to a bowl and let cool.

In another bowl, dissolve the yeast in the warm water and add the sugar.

When the tomato pulp mixture is cooled, beat in the egg and stir in the dissolved yeast mixture. Gradually work in the flour until you have a smooth dough.

Cover the dough in the bowl with a dry cloth and set in a warm place to rise until doubled in volume, approximately 1 hour. Punch down the dough and turn it out onto a floured pastry board. Knead for 2 minutes or until you have a smooth and elastic dough. Roll the dough out to ½" thickness and cut into 12 rolls. Preheat the oven to 400 degrees.

Place the rolls on a greased baking sheet, cover with a dry towel, and let stand again in a warm place until doubled in bulk, approximately 40 minutes. Bake the rolls in the oven for 12 minutes or until done. Serve hot. Makes 1 dozen.

TOMATO SORBET

**1 cup fresh tomato juice (see Simple Raw
    Tomato Juice), at room temperature**
1½ cup granulated sugar
½ cup warm water
2 oz. vodka or rum
1 large egg white
2 tbsp. powdered sugar

In a bowl, combine the tomato juice, sugar, and warm water. Stir together until the sugar is completely dissolved and the mixture is syrupy.

Stir in the vodka or rum and pour the mixture into a container and place in the freezer for an hour or more.

Seat a mixing bowl over a saucepan of warm water (about 150 degrees) and beat the egg white with the powdered sugar until the mixture is stiff and silken.

Carefully fold ⅓ of the egg white mixture at a time into the softly frozen sorbet base from the freezer, transfer to a freezer container, cover, and freeze for 2 hours, or until the Tomato Sorbet is properly set. Makes approximately 1 quart.

TOMATO CAKE
WITH TOMATO BUTTERCREAM ICING

¾ cup tomato puree from very ripe tomatoes
¼ cup (4 tbsp.) Tomato Paste
2 tbsp. sour cream
2 large eggs
2 tsp. grated lemon zest
1½ tsp. vanilla extract
2 cups presifted all-purpose flour
1¼ cups sugar
1 tsp. baking soda
1 tsp. baking powder
½ cup salted butter, softened

Preheat the oven to 350 degrees.

Butter a 9" x 2" cake pan or 9" springform pan and line it with parchment or waxed paper. Butter the paper and dust it with flour.

In a food processor, process the tomato puree, Tomato Paste, and sour cream until smooth. Add the eggs, grated lemon zest, and vanilla extract and process until well blended.

In a mixing bowl, combine the flour, sugar, baking soda, and baking powder. Add the butter and half of the tomato mixture. Beat together until well blended. Add half of the remaining tomato mixture, blending it in thoroughly before adding the rest. Continue beating until all is well blended.

Scrape the batter into the buttered baking pan and smooth the top surface with a spatula. Bake for 30 minutes, or until a knife inserted into the cake comes out clean.

Remove the tomato cake from the oven and place it on a wire rack to cool for about 15 minutes. Loosen the cake from the sides of the pan with a knife and remove the cake from the pan. Place the cake on the wire rack and let it cool completely before serving or icing. Makes 1 cake.

TOMATO BUTTERCREAM ICING

6 large egg yolks
1 cup sugar
½ cup corn syrup
1 tsp. vanilla extract
2 lb. unsalted butter
⅓ cup Tomato Paste
Red food coloring, optional

In a mixing bowl, beat the egg yolks with an electric mixer until they are pale yellow in color.

In a small saucepan on the stove, combine the sugar and corn syrup and stir until the sugar is completely melted and the syrup comes to a rolling boil. Pour the hot syrup into a glass measuring cup or heatproof bowl to stop the cooking.

Pour the syrup into the yolks in a steady stream until all has been incorporated. Don't pour the syrup onto the beaters or it will end up on the sides of your mixing bowl rather than in your mixture. To do this, pour small amounts at a time into the mixture and beat in each amount as it is added. Continue beating until the mixture is completely cool.

Add the vanilla extract and gradually beat in the softened butter in about 6 batches. Add the Tomato Paste and continue beating until all is well incorporated. If you would like a redder color, beat in a few drops of red food coloring here until it reaches the intensity of red you want.

Use the Tomato Buttercream to ice the Tomato Cake immediately, or store the buttercream in a tightly covered bowl in the refrigerator. If the buttercream is refrigerated before using, allow it to come to room temperature before icing the cake.

Note: The corn syrup can be the clear Karo type, or may be more extravagant and deliver a more intense flavor if a rich sugarcane syrup such as Steen's is used.

Do not heat the buttercream after it has been refrigerated to bring it to room temperature. It will separate. The buttercream can, however, be beaten again in the mixer to bring it back to the light fluffy texture that may have been lost somewhat in the refrigeration storage.

It may sound odd to think of tomato as the flavor of a sweet buttercream icing, but why not? Lemon, too, would be a strange flavor for a sweet dessert if it were not for the sweetness of sugar. Tomatoes are not just for salads anymore!

GREEN TOMATO PIE

1 cup sugar
½ cup brown sugar
2 tsp. ground cinnamon
1 tsp. ground ginger
5 cups skinned (well packed), seeded, sliced,
and drained green tomatoes cut into eighths.
1 Double Pie Crust (see below), or 2 frozen pie crusts
2 tbsp. butter
1 egg, separated
1 tbsp. water
1 tbsp. milk
2 tbsp. sugar
¼ tsp. ground cinnamon

Preheat the oven to 425 degrees.

In a bowl, combine the sugar, brown sugar, cinnamon, and ginger. Add the tomato slices and fold all together well. Transfer the tomato mixture to the cooked pie shell, along with the liquids in the bowl. Dot the tomato mixture with the 2 tbsp. butter.

Beat the egg white slightly with the water. Paint the rim of the cooked pie crust with the egg white wash and rest the upper crust layer over the filled crust. Press the edges to seal the two crusts together.

Beat the egg yolk with the milk. Paint the top crust with the egg yolk wash. Sprinkle the top crust with the 2 tbsp. white sugar and a little more powdered cinnamon. Cut short slits in the top crust in several places to release the steam during the cooking. Place the pie on a cookie sheet in the center of the preheated oven for 15 minutes, turn the oven down to 350 degrees, and bake for an additional 30 minutes. Makes 1 9" deep-dish, double-crust pie.

DOUBLE PIE CRUST, PARTIALLY PREBAKED

3 cups presifted all-purpose flour
2 tbsp. brown sugar
½ tsp. ground cinnamon
½ tsp. salt
1 cup salted butter
½ cup cold water

Preheat the oven to 400 degrees.

In a bowl or on a pastry board, mix together the flour, brown sugar, cinnamon, and salt. Blend the butter into the mixture by breaking it into small pieces and working it into the flour until it is crumbly as coarse meal. Make a well in the middle of the dough and add the cold water, 2 tbsp. at a time. Work it in to bind the dough and knead until smooth. Work quickly on a cool surface so the butter does not melt. If the dough becomes too soft, refrigerate it for 15 minutes to stiffen it up a bit.

Cut the dough in half and roll into two balls. Wrap one dough ball in plastic wrap and set aside, or refrigerate if it needs firming up. Place the other dough ball on a lightly floured surface and roll it out in a circle that extends two inches wider than the 9" pie pan. Roll the dough up onto the rolling pin and unroll it onto the buttered pie pan. Fit it into the pan and cut off the edges around the outside of the pan rim with a knife.

Prick the dough all around the sides and bottom with a fork. Lay a piece of foil into the dough and fill it with dried beans or small washed pebbles to weight down the crust during the cooking. Bake in the oven for 10-12 minutes.

Remove the partially baked pie crust from the oven and remove the foil and beans from the crust. Allow to cool on a wire rack for at least 15 minutes before filling. After filling, roll out the remaining dough and cover pie. Makes 1 double 9" pie crust.

Note: This pie is that it is not too sweet, yet it satisfies as a sweet dessert. With ice cream it does become more dessertish, while alone it makes a nice sort of afternoon pie, or even a nice breakfast pie, for a change of pace.

If you want a more wintery pie, try the addition or increase of these ingredients: ½ cup white granulated sugar, 1½ tsp. vanilla extract, 1 tsp. cinnamon, ¼ tsp. ginger, ¼ tsp. allspice, and ¼ tsp. cloves.

The tomatoes should be green to ensure that their texture holds up in the cooking. Unripe reddening tomatoes will work as well.

Index

African groundnut sauce, 149
African seafood stew, 118-19
African tomato and potato curry, 97
Andalusian tomato and rice salad, 59
Antibes sauce, 150
Aurora sauce, 150-51
Avignon tomato and eggplant casserole, 88

Bacon and tomato muffins, 179-80
Baked eggs in tomatoes, 103
Baked oysters Thermidor, 37
Baked tomato and corn casserole, 87
Baltic tomatoes, 29
Balsamic vinegar steamed salmon fillets with tomatoes and onions, 120-21
Bean curd with tomato and beef, stir-fried, 145
Beaulieu, tomatoes, 35
Beauregard, tomatoes, 31
Beef
    daube of, 141
    sauce tujague, boiled, 152
    stir-fried bean curd with tomato and, 145
    stock, 151
Beer, tomato, 20
Beignets, crabmeat, with tomato sauce, 38
Bisque(s)
    tomato cream, with sherry, 51
    Louisiana tomato, 47
    tomato and crab, 49
    tomato and eggplant, 50
Black bean and tomato soup, 55
Black beans and tomatoes, Caribbean, 98
Bloody bull, 21
Bloody Mary, 21
Bloody Mary, Cajun, 22
Bloody Mary, Caribbean, 22
Bloody Mary, Creole, 24
Bloody Mary, Mexican, 25
Bloody Mary with horseradish, Gulf coast, 23
Bon ton sauce, 151
Boiled beef sauce tujague, 152
Brazilian chicken and tomato soup, 46
Brazilian stewed okra with tomatoes, 82-83
Brazilian tomato and shrimp rice, 119

Breaded pan-fried fish fillets with crayfish Creole, 125
Broiled tomatoes with black olives and Romano cheese, 76
Broiled tomatoes with bread crumbs, 75
Butter, tomato, 160

Cajun bloody Mary, 22
Cake, tomato, with tomato buttercream icing, 184-85
Canapé, sardines Rovigo, 32
Cantonese tomato and beef soup, 56
Caribbean black beans and tomatoes, 98
Caribbean bloody Mary, 22
Caribbean curried tomato, corn, orange, and onion salad, 60-61
Caribbean curry-lime dressing, 61
Caribbean fish, tomato, avocado, and grapefruit salad, 62
Caribbean tomato-pineapple jam, 172
Catsup, tomato, 169
Ceviche, 34-35
Chicken
    Andalusian, grilled, 133
    and mushrooms, tomatoes stuffed with, 63
    and tomato hoppin' John, 134-35
    and tomato salad, Creole, 65
    and tomato maque choux, 135
    aurora, poached, 132
    breast with Creole sauce en papillote, 136
    Creole, 131
    Marengo, 137-38
Chili tomato rice with petits pois, 92-93
Chilled egg-stuffed tomatoes, 64-65
Chinese stir-fried cabbage with tomato, 97-98
Chinese stir-fried tomatoes in egg sauce, 84-85
Chutney
    green tomato, 170-71
    green tomato-mango, 170
    pineapple-tomato, 171
Clam chowder, Manhattan, 52-53
Cocktail sauce, 152

Cocktail, tequila sangrita, 24-25
Cocktail, tomato-clam, 20
Colbert sauce, 152
Collards with tomatoes and coconut milk,
    Kenyan, 89-90
Cold tomato and sweet potato soup, 51-52
Cold tomato mousse, 33
Cooked tomato juice, 19
Corn casserole, baked tomato and, 87
Corn muffins, tomato jam, 181
Corn muffins, tomato preserve, 181
Corn muffins, tomato spice, 182
Court bouillon, redfish, 116
Crab(meat)
    beignets with tomato sauce, 38
    bisque, tomato and, 49
    ravigote, tomato, 40-41
Crayfish Creole, 113
Crayfish Creole, breaded pan-fried fish fillets
    with, 125
Creole bloody Mary, 24
Creole, chicken, 131
Creole chicken and tomato salad, 65
Creole sauce, 154-55
Criolla salsa, 167
Cypriote sauce, 153

Daube of beef, 141
Demi-glas sauce, 155
Double pie crust, partially prebaked, 187
Dressing(s)
    Caribbean curry-lime, 61
    Russian tomato, 68-69, 157
    tomatette, 160
Dumplings, tomato bisque, 48

Egg(s)
    and tomato sandwich, 105
    in tomatoes, baked, 103
    Mireille, fried, 103-4
    Mistral, fried, 104
    Portuguese scrambled, 105-6
    salad, Roma tomato and, 64
    -stuffed tomatoes, chilled, 64-65
Eggplant bisque, tomato and, 50
Eggplant casserole, Avignon tomato and, 88

Fillet of fish en papillote, 126-27
Fish
    en papillote, fillet of, 126-27

fillets Andalouse, grilled, 115
fillets simmered in tomato and leek sauce,
    114
fillets with crayfish Creole, breaded
pan-fried, 125
poaching liquor, 117
ragout, tomato, 111
salad, Caribbean, avocado and
    grapefruit, 62
stock, 156
tomato, and pepper soup, West
African, 53
Ugandan steamed, 123
Flaming tomato punch, 26
Flounder, tomato-stuffed, 124
Fresh green tomato relish, 174-75
Fribourg, tomato, 34
Fried eggs Mireille, 103-4
Fried eggs Mistral, 104
Fried tomatoes in cracker crumbs, 77

Gazpacho, tomato, mango, and avocado, 45
Ghana stewed tomatoes with spinach with
    pork, 146
Green tomato and mustard pickle, 175
Green tomato chutney, 170-71
Green tomato jam, 172
Green tomato pie, 186-87
Green tomato-mango chutney, 170
Green tomato relish, fresh, 174-75
Green tomatoes, horseradish pickled, 174
Grill-roasted tomatoes, 79
Grilled chicken Andalusian, 133
Grilled fish fillets Andalouse, 115
Grilled marinated tomatoes, 79
Grilled redfish with Criolla salsa, 121
Grilled Roma tomatoes with fresh dill,
    80-81
Grilled shrimp and tomatoes on skewers,
    122-23
Grilled tomato rounds, 78
Grits, tomato, 86
Guacamole, tomato, 36
Gulf coast bloody Mary with horseradish, 23

Hoppin' John, chicken and tomato, 134-35
Horseradish pickled green tomatoes, 174
Huevos rancheros, 106

Icing, tomato buttercream, 185

Indian tomato, red onion, and ginger salad, 66
Italian sweet tomato preserves, 173

Jam
    Caribbean tomato-pineapple, 172
    green tomato, 172
    tomato-papaya, with ginger, 173
Jeannette, tomatoes, 75
Juice, cooked tomato, 19
Juice, simple raw tomato, 19

Kenyan collards with tomatoes and coconut milk, 89-90

Louisiana tomato bisque, 47

Macaroni Neapolitan, 100
Madeira sauce, 156
Manhattan clam chowder, 52-53
Maque choux, chicken and tomato, 135
Mayonnaise, 158-59
Mayonnaise, tomato, 158
Mexican bloody Mary, 25
Mexican salsa, 167
Mireille, tomatoes, 90
Mousse, cold tomato, 33
Muffins
    bacon and tomato, 179-80
    tomato, 179
    tomato jam corn, 181
    tomato-pecan, 180
    tomato preserve corn, 181
    tomato spice corn, 182

Nigerian tomato and fruit salad, 72
Nigerian tomato and pumpkin seed soup, 54

Oaxacan picadillo, 143
Okra and tomatoes, stewed, 82
Okra, Brazilian stewed, with tomatoes, 82-83
Onions, scalloped tomatoes and, 89
Osso bucco Milanese, 144
Oysters Thermidor, baked, 37

Pan-fried breaded tomatoes, 76-77
Paste, tomato, 162-63
Picadillo-stuffed tomato in salsa roja, 142-43
Pie, green tomato, 186-87

Pie crust, double, partially prebaked, 187
Pineapple-tomato chutney, 171
Poached chicken aurora, 132
Poached red snapper with aurora sauce, 117
Poaching liquor (for fish), 117
Portuguese scrambled eggs, 105-6
Potato curry, African tomato and, 97
Poydras sauce, 156
Preserves, Italian sweet tomato, 173

Ravigote, tomato crabmeat, 40-41
Red snapper with aurora sauce, Poached, 117
Red wine sauce, tomato, 164
Redfish with Criolla salsa, grilled, 121
Redfish court bouillon, 116
Relish, fresh green tomato, 174-75
Relish, tomato and corn, 176
Rice, Brazilian tomato and shrimp, 119
Rice salad, Andalusian tomato and, 59
Rice, tomato, 85
Rice with petits pois, chili tomato, 92-93
Roasted Anaheim chili and tomato sauce, 157
Roasted tomato salad with tarragon, 71
Roasted tomatoes, 84
Rolls, tomato yeast, 182-83
Roma tomato and egg salad, 64
Roma tomato rings stuffed with cream cheese, 30
Roma tomatoes with fresh dill, grilled, 80-81
Russian tomato dressing, 68-69, 157

Salad
    Andalusian tomato and rice, 59
    Caribbean curried tomato, corn, orange, and onion, 60-61
    Caribbean fish, tomato, avocado, and grapefruit, 62
    Creole chicken and tomato, 65
    dressing,
        curry-lime, Caribbean, 61
        Russian tomato, 68-69, 157
        tomatette, 66
    Indian tomato, red onion, and ginger, 66
    Nigerian tomato and fruit, 72
    roasted tomato, with tarragon, 71
    Roma tomato and egg, 64
    tomato, avocado, and red onion, with Russian tomato dressing, 67-69

tomato ball, 69
tomato, with olive-anchovy dressing,
    71-72
tomato, with tomatette dressing, 66
Yugoslavian tomato and pepper, with
    goat cheese, 67
Salmon fillets with tomatoes and onions,
    balsamic vinegar steamed, 120-21
Salsa
    Criolla, 167
    tomato, 168
    tomato and red onion, 168
    Yucatecan tomato and habanero, 169
Sandwich, egg and tomato, 105
Sardines Rovigo canapé, 32
Sauce(s)
    African groundnut, 149
    Andalouse, 149
    Antibes, 150
    Aurora, 150-51
    bon ton, 151
    Cocktail, 152
    Colbert, 152
    Creole, 154-55
    Cypriote, 153
    demi-glas, 155
    Madeira, 156
    Poydras, 156
    roasted Anaheim chili and tomato, 157
    Spanish, 159
    tomatette dressing, 160
    tomato, 161
    tomato and chili, 161
    tomato clam, 162
    tomato paste, 162
    tomato red wine, 163
    Tujague, boiled beef, 152
    velouté, with fish fume and white wine,
        164
Scalloped tomatoes and onions, 89
Shrimp
    and tomatoes on skewers, grilled, 122-23
    Creole, 112
    fillet of fish en papillote, 126
    remoulade, tomato, 39
Simple raw tomato juice, 19
Sorbet, tomato, 183
Soufflé casserole, tomato, 107
Soup(s)
    black bean and tomato, 55

Brazilian chicken and tomato, 46
Cantonese tomato and beef, 56
clam chowder, Manhattan, 52-53
cold tomato and sweet potato, 51-52
Louisiana tomato bisque, 47
Nigerian tomato and pumpkin seed, 54
tomato and eggplant bisque, 50
tomato cream bisque with sherry, 51
tomato, mango, and avocado gazpacho,
    45
West African fish, tomato, and pepper,
    53
Spanish sauce, 159
Spanish tomatoes, 70
Steamed tomatoes, 83
Stew, African seafood, 118-19
Stewed okra and tomatoes, 82
Stewed tomatoes, 81
Stewed tomatoes and spinach with pork,
    Ghana, 146
Stir-fried bean curd with tomato and beef,
    145
Stir-fried cabbage with tomato, Chinese,
    97-98
Stir-fried tomatoes in egg sauce, Chinese,
    84-85
Stock, beef, 151
Stock, fish, 153
Sweet potato soup, cold tomato and,
    51-52

Tequila sangrita cocktail, 24
Thermidor, baked oysters, 37
Tomatette dressing, 160
Tomato(es)
    and beef soup, Cantonese, 56
    and chili sauce, 161
    and corn casserole, baked, 87
    and corn relish, 176
    and crab bisque, 49
    and eggplant bisque, 50
    and eggplant casserole, Avignon, 88
    and habanero salsa, Yucatecan, 169
    and mustard pickle, green, 175
    and onions, scalloped, 89
    and pepper soup, West African fish, 53
    and potato curry, African, 97
    and pumpkin seed soup, Nigerian, 54
    and red onion salsa, 168
    and shrimp rice, Brazilian, 119

and spinach with pork, Ghana stewed, 146
and sweet potato soup, cold, 51-52
avocado, and red onion salad with Russian tomato dressing, 67-69
ball salad, 69
Baltic, 29
Beaulieu, 35
Beauregard, 31
beer, 20
bisque dumplings, 48
bisque, Louisiana, 47
broiled, with black olives and Romano cheese, 76
broiled, with bread crumbs, 75
butter, 160
buttercream icing, 185
cake with tomato buttercream icing, 184-85
catsup, 169
chilled egg-stuffed, 64-65
-clam cocktail, 20
clam sauce, 162
crabmeat ravigote, 40
cream bisque with sherry, 51
fish ragout, 111
Fribourg, 34
fried, in cracker crumbs, 77
grill-roasted, 79
grilled marinated, 79
grits, 86
guacamole, 36
in egg sauce, Chinese stir-fried, 84-85
jam, green, 172
jam corn muffins, 181
Jeannette, 75
mango, and avocado gazpacho, 45
mayonnaise, 158-59
Mireille, 90-91
mousse, cold, 33
muffins, 179
pan-fried breaded, 76-77
-papaya jam with ginger, 173
paste, 162-63
-pecan muffins, 180
pie, green, 186-87
-pineapple jam, Caribbean, 172

Portuguese, 91
preserve corn muffins, 181
preserves, Italian sweet, 173
punch, flaming, 26
red wine sauce, 163
relish, fresh green, 174-75
rice, 85
rice, white beans with tomatoes and, 99 100
rings stuffed with cream cheese, Roma, 30
roasted, 84
rounds, grilled, 78
salad with olive-anchovy dressing, 71-72
salad with tomatette dressing, 66
salsa, 168
sauce, 161
sauce, roasted Anaheim chili and, 157
shrimp remoulade, 39
sorbet, 183
soufflé casserole, 107
soup, black bean and, 55
Spanish, 70
spice corn muffins, 182
steamed, 83
stewed, 81
-stuffed flounder, 124
stuffed with chicken and mushrooms, 63
whole grilled, 80
yeast rolls, 182-83

Ugandan sautéed mixed vegetables, 93
Ugandan steamed fish, 123

Vegetables, Ugandan sautéed mixed, 93
Velouté sauce with fish fume and white wine, 164

West African fish, tomato, and pepper soup, 53
White beans with tomatoes and tomato rice, 99-100
Whole grilled tomatoes, 80

Yucatecan tomato and habanero salsa, 169
Yugoslavian tomato and pepper salad with goat cheese, 67